PENGUIN BOOKS

GOD'S FARTHEST OUTPOST

MICHAEL KING is one of New Zealand's leading biographers and historians. Like the majority of New Zealand Catholics he is of predominantly Irish descent. He was educated in Catholic schools in the years immediately prior to the Second Vatican Council. For the past three decades he has worked as an author, journalist, broadcaster, teacher and commentator on social and cultural affairs. Dr King welcomed the invitation to write this book as 'an opportunity to explore my own cultural and religious heritage – one that has largely been neglected by mainstream historical writing in New Zealand'.

Service at St Joseph's - Dunedin

GOD'S FARTHEST OUTPOST

A History Of Catholics In New New Zealand

MICHAEL KING

(Research by Merle van de Klundert)

PENGUIN BOOKS

PENGUIN
Penguin Books (NZ) Ltd, Cnr Rosedale and Airborne Roads, Albany, Auckland 1310, New Zealand
Penguin Books Ltd, 27 Wrights Lane, London W8 5TZ, England
Penguin USA, 375 Hudson Street, New York, NY 10014, United States
Penguin Books Australia Ltd, 487 Maroondah Highway, Ringwood, Australia 3134
Penguin Books Canada Ltd, 10 Alcorn Avenue, Toronto, Ontario, Canada M4V 3B2

Penguin Books Ltd, Registered Offices: Harmondsworth, Middlesex, England

First published by Penguin Books (NZ) Ltd, 1997

1 3 5 7 9 10 8 6 4 2

Design & Production by Maria Jungowska/Scope
Typeset in Berkeley
Printed in Singapore

Frontispiece ~ Evening service at Saint Joseph's Catholic Cathedral, Dunedin, 1890. From a watercolour painting by William Mathew Hodgkins.
Alexander Turnbull Library

For pathfinders and mentors ~
Maurice Mulcahy, Frank McKay, Ernest Simmons,
John Dunmore, Mick O'Meeghan, Hugh Laracy,
Patrick O'Farrell, Henare Tate and Manuka Henare

❖

'We could have gone almost anywhere in the world, wherever we had missions. Some of our people liked the thought of Africa, or India. But I wanted to go to New Zealand. It was as far away as you could get from Europe, going east or west; or from the Holy Land. In my mind it was God's farthest outpost . . .'

Father Theo Wanders MHM

❖

CONTENTS

BY THE SAME AUTHOR

Moko, Maori Tattooing in the Twentieth Century
Make It News, How to Approach the Media
Te Ao Hurihuri (Ed.)
Te Puea
Tihei Mauri Ora (Ed.)
New Zealand, Its Land and Its People
New Zealanders at War
The Collector, A Biography of Andreas Reischek
A Place to Stand, A History of Turangawaewae Marae
New Zealand in Colour
Apirana Ngata, Colossus of Maoridom
Maori, A Photographic and Social History
Whina, A Biography of Whina Cooper
Being Pakeha, An Encounter with New Zealand and the Maori Renaissance
Kawe Korero, A Guide to Reporting Maori Activities
Auckland
Death of the Rainbow Warrior
New Zealand
After the War, New Zealand Since 1945
One of the Boys? Changing Views of Masculinity in New Zealand (Ed.)
Moriori, A People Rediscovered
A Land Apart, The Chatham Islands of New Zealand
Pakeha, The Quest for Identity in New Zealand (Ed.)
Hidden Places, A Memoir in Journalism
The Coromandel
Frank Sargeson, A Life

FOREWORD

A historian could cite a variety of dates for the origins of the Catholic Church in New Zealand. Bishop Pompallier and the first of his band of Marist missionaries reached the country in 1838. Eight years earlier New Zealand was mentioned for the first time in an official Church document, that defining the responsibilities of the Prefect Apostolic of the South Seas and placing its islands in what was, in effect, the largest diocese in the world.

For the purpose of this book the story of Catholics in New Zealand begins at the point where they first set foot in the country, in 1769. And the Church has had a continuous presence there from the time of permanent settlement by Irish Catholics in the 1820s and the first conversions of Maori in the 1830s.

Where to end is equally debatable, given that the history of the Church in New Zealand is far from finished. I have closed the narrative at the point where reforms initiated by the Second Vatican Council were about to affect New Zealand in the early 1960s. That process provided a break with the continuities of the previous 130 years; and it is difficult to impose historical perspective on a recent and controversial period of rapid change. The post-Vatican II Church in New Zealand is largely, then, another story for another occasion — though I have summarised some of its major features in an epilogue.

While, inevitably, bishops, priests and members of religious orders figure prominently in this book, their experience is not that of the Church as a whole. As Father Ernest Simmons has noted, the history of Catholics in New Zealand is a story of a multitude of men, women and children of many cultures — Maori, French, Irish, English, Scots, Italians, Poles, Bohemians, Serbs, Croats, Dutch, Pacific Islanders and others. To be Catholic, Father Simmons goes on to say, is to inherit and hold 'a set of beliefs and practices which are reflected and expressed in a way of life. The . . . customs and way of looking at the world which make Catholics different from other people are not static, but they do make Catholics in New Zealand an identifiable community . . .'

This book, in text and photographs, is the story of that community from the 1830s to the 1960s. As a novice in the field of Church history I am indebted to the people who helped me tell it: their names are recorded with profound gratitude in the acknowledgments.

Michael King

PROLOGUE

Being Catholic ~ A Memoir

'There is a moment in all religions,' Edmund Campion writes, 'when the present falls away and you are standing in eternity.'[1] And that, indeed, is a description of the most universal experience religions offer: that of giving life on the physical plane resonances of the spiritual and the eternal. Some people encounter such intimations in deep accord with the natural world, some in worshipping under stone arches in medieval cathedrals, and some in praying with head bowed and eyes closed in a Huntly-brick bedroom in suburbia.

For me that experience has been felt most intensely at prayer and song in a buttressed wooden-Gothic church on Taiao Hill overlooking Whangape Harbour in Northland. Saint Gabriel's was built of kauri in the late nineteenth century at a time when Whangape was a trading port and a timber mill operated on the northern shore. Now it survives as a monument to spirituality against a backdrop of hills, estuary, cabbage trees and macrocarpas — a landscape that is largely devoid of evidence of human occupation.

That juxtaposition of nature and spirituality is part of the church's appeal. So is the fact that on Sundays it fills with people,

Opposite ~ Saint Gabriel's Church, Pawarenga ~ a place of pilgrimage and a quintessentially New Zealand monument to spirituality.
~ *Robin Morrison*

most of them members of the Uri-o-Tai hapu of Te Rarawa. They worship in Maori and the building vibrates with the harmonies of hymns and prayers. After Mass the congregation gathers outside to talk in the sun among the graves of ancestors.

The view is redolent of Maori and Christian Maori associations. The hill on which the church stands is the site of a decisive battle between Ngapuhi and Ngati Ruanui, who changed their name to Te Aupouri ('the smokescreen') to commemorate the fact that they escaped from Makora pa on Taio Hill under a pall of smoke. One of the graves is that of Te Huhu, ariki of Pawarenga and one of the first Maori baptised by Bishop Pompallier. Looking across the water and back up the Pawarenga Valley it is possible to see a total of four churches. And one is aware that, in Maori cosmology, this part of the country was Te Hiku-o-te-Ika, the Tail of Maui's Fish, over which souls pass on their way to Te Rerenga Wairua, the Leaping-Off Place of the dead. For Catholic Maori there are no contradictions in these associations. They are all part of wairua Maori, Maori spirituality.

For a Pakeha person they have slightly different connotations. Saint Gabriel's and its surrounding landscape put me in mind of Ireland, the Hawaiiki-nui or Homeland for most non-Maori Catholics in New Zealand. The auld sod too is littered with monuments to spirituality, though of a more permanent kind: dolmens, circles of standing stones, ruins of monasteries, round towers and Celtic crosses — all of which speak of a glorious past in which ancestors were saints or kings and sometimes both.

Worshipping inside Saint Gabriel's, bathed in the amber light that reflects off its kauri walls, also reminds me of another wooden country building, Saint Michael's in Pauatahanui, where I went to Mass as a child. I wrote in *Being Pakeha*:

'That church, built in local wood in 1878, stood alongside cabbage trees, kowhais and macrocarpas on a hillside above Stace's Flat. In spring and summer the sacristy doors were thrown open and we could see grass and trees behind the altar. Families who had built the church — the Abbotts and the Murphys — had their own pews. The windows were papered with peeling pictures of Christ and an assortment of saints. The wood of the walls and pews was stained dark with age and varnish . . . I could never again smell incense or burning candles without that simple solid building and its occupants coming forcefully to mind . . .'[2]

There is a further reason why Saint Gabriel's and its surroundings are precious to me. In such an environment, where few signs of the twentieth century intrude, the past seems to lie close to the present; the psychic residue of previous human activities and emotions is strong. On a crystalline morning one experiences what my Irish grandmother used to call a 'trembling of the veil'.

Priest as hero ~ Father Patrick Mackay, who married my maternal grandparents. One of the many sacerdotal portraits that cluttered my Irish grandmother's house.
~ *Michael King*

Somewhere there, just a little beyond sight and hearing, it is almost possible to make out the figure of French Marist Catherin Servant, who foot-slogged his way up here from the Hokianga before 1840; or the Italian Franciscans who followed him on horseback in the 1860s; or the wild-looking Irishman James McDonald, Maketanara, who criss-crossed the valley in the 1880s like a prophet from the Old Testament; or the German Mill Hill priest John Becker, who encouraged his Pawarenga parishioners to erect Saint Gabriel's high on Taiao Hill so that it might bear spectacular witness to their Faith.

All these men are remembered still at Pawarenga. And all the associations generated by that particular church remind one that feelings of spirituality are almost always a complex interaction between our past and present lives, and often between our own lives and those of our ancestors; and that Catholicism has been long enough established in New Zealand to build up an accretion of events, memories and associations that we call history. For those of us who are old enough, that history is divided between the pre- and post-Vatican II eras as surely as if by a hinge.

Saint Patrick's Day processions, given impetus by 'the Troubles' in Ireland, were a feature of my mother's childhood. This one took place in Greymouth in 1918.
~ *Tom Duffy*

Like those of most New Zealand Catholics, my forebears came out of Ireland.* My mother's grandfather, Peter Tierney, left Roos in County Mayo in 1856 after a wild quarrel with his father. My father's great-grandfather, John Crawley, abandoned Newry in County Armagh at the height of the Famine in the late 1840s.

Neither ancestor came to New Zealand. The Tierneys established themselves at Hexham-on-Tyne in the north of England; the Crawleys and the family with whom they intermarried, the Cassidys, in industrial Glasgow. There they found employment and sustenance in greater measure than they had known in Ireland. But they also encountered sectarianism every bit as sharp as that which had existed between Catholics and plantation Protestants back home. A cousin of my father's remembers their grandmother, Mary Crawley, stockpiling chamberpots of urine to toss on the Orangemen's Walk below her tenement window on 12 July, the anniversary of the Battle of the Boyne, when Protestants celebrated the suppression of Irish culture, religion and language.

In the New Zealand to which both families had migrated by the 1920s the sectarianism was there still, though muted. A 'hard bigoted Ulsterman', William Ferguson Massey, was Prime

**Donald Akenson has called the constituency of the Catholic Church in New Zealand 'overwhelmingly Irish' and estimates that even by 1945 the Pakeha membership of the Church was 95 percent Irish in origin (Akenson 1990, p.162).*

Minister.[3] He had defeated the Catholic and Irish-descended Joe Ward. And the Protestant Political Association, whipped up to periodic frenzies by its leader the Rev. Howard Elliott, was at the height of its campaign against 'rum, Romanism and rebellion'. In those days of 'the Troubles' that followed the Easter 1916 uprising in Dublin, the PPA regarded any assertion of Irishness or Catholicity in New Zealand as tantamount to disloyalty to England and Empire. My Aunt Mona, told to write a homework composition on the significance of the Union Jack, proposed:

> Red is the colour of the blood we've shed
> In making England's name.
> White as the snow have our motives been
> In spreading England's fame.
> Blue is the colour of our naval lads,
> The finest that the world has ever seen.
> And if you want another colour to compare with all the rest,
> Old Ireland sends its little bit of green.[4]

The headmaster of Porirua School, a PPA stalwart, was not pleased. He read the pieces out to morning assembly but, looking thunderous, omitted my aunt's last two lines. My mother did rather better. At the school concert the same year she sang 'The Dear

Opening day at Saint Brigid's Convent School, Johnsonville, February 1929 ~ uniforms not yet standardised.
~ *Michael King*

Parish picnic, Plimmerton, 1920 ~ my mother holding sun hat in front left-hand corner.
~ *Michael King*

Little Shamrock'. Her godmother, Annie O'Malley, dressed her in a green sateen frock, green stockings and green shoes. She was wired with three green paper leaves, one behind her head, the others on each arm. When she raised both arms as she sang, she *became* a shamrock.

Porirua was at that time part of the Lower Hutt parish, which included Pauatahanui, Plimmerton and Johnsonville. The parish priests, Dean Lane and Father Michael Griffin, were Irish. The family's favourite curate, Father Jim Henley, had Irish parents. The Brigidine nuns, who opened a convent at Johnsonville in time for my mother to attend in her last year of primary school, were Irish. Some of the men of the parish belonged to the Hibernians. The social highlights of the year were Saint Patrick's Day — with its parade, sports and evening concert in Wellington — and the parish picnic at Plimmerton Beach. To be Catholic then was to live in a subculture of the Irish diaspora.

Thirty years later when I went to Saint Theresa's Convent School in Plimmerton — now, with Pauatahanui, an independent parish — it seemed to my mother that little had changed. In the early 1950s our priests were still Irish (Fathers Jeremiah McGrath and Bill Clancy); the nuns who taught us, Sisters of Saint Joseph of Nazareth, were not — but they were largely the daughters and granddaughters of Irish migrants.

Prayer to a Guardian Angel

Angel of God
My guardian dear,
To whom God's love
Commits me here.

Ever this day
Be at my side,
To light and guard,
To rule and guide.
Amen

Six foot four inches of Father Jeremiah McGrath towers over Pat Lawlor at Plimmerton, early 1950s.
~ Pat Lawlor Collection

The Faith communicated to us was, as it had been from the time the Irish set foot in New Zealand, a mixture of worship, formal Church teaching (via the Catechism), superstition and Celtic mythology. We were assured by the nuns, for example, that the souls in Purgatory would haunt us if we failed to pray for their deliverance (and Miss Balotti, the priests' housekeeper, insisted on an exorcism in the presbytery when she was pursued by a particularly tenacious spirit). We were told that the end of the world would be prefigured by the disappearance of Ireland beneath the sea because God had promised to spare its people the fire and pain of Armageddon. We were warned that the Blessed Virgin had given a 'third message' to the children to whom she appeared at Fatima in 1917; it was so horrific that the Pope, when he read it, spent a full day walking around his garden chanting, 'No, no, no!' That message was to be made known to the world in 1960. (It was not: to our immense disappointment a Vatican

O God of goodness and mercy, take compassion on the souls of the faithful departed who are suffering in Purgatory; put an end to their torments, and grant especially to those for whom I am bound to pray, eternal life and rest.

spokesman revealed years later that the message was simply an 'education in faith'.)

When I contracted polio in 1955, in one of the last infantile paralysis epidemics, the girl from whom I caught it died. In great alarm Sister Isidore sent away to the order's mother house in Wanganui for the loan of a precious relic: a fragment of one of Saint Francis Xavier's leg bones. It was embedded in a silver cross with a tiny piece of glass at the centre, through which the sliver of holy bone was visible. Instructions were that the cross was to be pinned to my pyjama jacket as close as possible to my heart.

Saint Anthony ~ traditionally, the finder of lost treasures

When the relic arrived at Wellington Hospital I was delirious and have only the faintest memory of a nurse attaching it to me and telling me that it would make me better. I was disposed to believe it. Anything was preferable to the lumbar punctures (needles driven into the spine) which I seemed to have every day. A week later the delirium was over and I could again think and speak clearly. In gratitude I felt for the relic. It was gone. I summoned a nurse, but she had never seen it and searched my bedside locker fruitlessly. I prayed to Saint Anthony and wondered if the whole episode had been a dream; or a vision. But no: it turned out that the cross had disappeared into the hospital laundry when my pyjamas were changed. We never saw it again. But one of the doctors, trying to console me, did say that he thought the washing had turned out especially whiter and brighter that week, possibly as a result of miraculous intervention.

That same Sister Isidore, to whom I became especially close, taught the upper standards what she called 'Catholic history'. This included an explanation of the marvellous doctrine of the Communion of Saints. We, as baptised Catholics, shared spiritual goods with all the other Faithful on earth, with the souls suffering in Purgatory, and with the Church Triumphant in Heaven. Thus we were linked intimately to such great figures from the past as the Apostles, the Popes, Saint Patrick and the Celtic saints, the philosopher Thomas Aquinas, the artists of the Italian Renaissance and the writers Chesterton and Belloc; and to such New Zealand Church heroes as Mother Aubert and Father Emmet McHardy (whom my own dear Sister Isidore had also taught).

Sister Isidore told too the cautionary tales: the frightful deaths of Henry VIII and Elizabeth I, terrified that hell lay gaping to receive them because of their role in the English Reformation; and how God would have punished Oliver Cromwell's brutal suppression of all that gave meaning to the lives of the Irish. Much of this kind of instruction came by way of poetry. We learned about King Alfred's defeat of the pagan Danes, for example, through recitation of G. K. Chesterton's 'Ballad of the White Horse':

Sister Isidore of the 'Black Josephs', who threatened to haunt me if I neglected to become a priest.
~ Sisters of Saint Joseph

The high tide! King Alfred cried.
The high tide and the turn!
As a tide turns on the tall grey seas,
See how they waver in the trees,
How stray their spears, how knock their knees,
How wild their watchfires burn!

The Mother of God goes over them,
Walking on wind and flame,
And the storm-cloud drifts from city and dale,
And the White Horse stamps in the White Horse Vale,
And we shall yet drink Christian ale
In the village of our name.

The Mother of God goes over them,
On dreadful cherubs borne;

And the psalm is roaring above the rune,
And the cross goes over the sun and moon,
Endeth the battle of Ethandune
With the blowing of a horn.[5]

And the Christian defeat of the Saracens at Lepanto (this one read with a bamboo cane banging out the rhythm on the desk in front of her so that the effect was like a demented haka — a Christian haka):

Don John pounding from the slaughter-painted poop,
Purpling all the ocean like a bloody pirate's sloop,
Scarlet running over on the silvers and the golds,
Breaking of the hatches up and bursting of the holds,
Thronging of the thousands up that labour under sea,
White for bliss and blind for sun and stunned for liberty.

Vivat Hispania!
Domino Gloria!
Don John of Austria
has set his people free![6]

White-gloved, white-dressed and white-souled, friend and contemporary Juliet Mason (left) and Susan Moriarty make their First Communion at Saint Joseph's Church, New Plymouth, 1953.
~ Julie Park

Our sisters were known colloquially from the colour of their habit as the 'Black Joes' to distinguish them from Mother Mary MacKillop's 'Brown Joes'. Both orders had been established in Australia by Father Julian Tenison Woods and Mary MacKillop, and both taught in New Zealand. What you thought of Mother MacKillop and Father Woods depended on which order you were taught by. Our received wisdom was that Father Woods was a mild and saintly man whom Mary MacKillop had attempted to outmanoeuvre. Pupils of the Brown Saint Joes had a different version and won a huge tactical victory when Mother MacKillop was beatified in Sydney forty years later.

The Australian roots of both congregations were reinforced by the sisters' fondness for another book of poems, *Around the Boree Log* by John O'Brien, who was in fact the 'bush priest' Father Patrick Hartigan. From him, via Sister Isidore, we learned about McEvoy the altar boy, aged 'sixty come November'; about the 'day before the races at Tangmalangaloo'; and about that example to us all — but especially to the girls among us — the 'Little Irish Mother':

There's a Little Irish Mother that a lonely vigil keeps
In the settler's hut where seldom stranger comes,
Watching by the home-made cradle where one more Australian sleeps

While the breezes whisper weird things to the gums
Where the settlers battle gamely, beaten down to rise again,
And the brave bush wives the toil and silence share,
Where the nation is a-building in the hearts of splendid men
There's a Little Irish Mother always there.[7]

Another example held up constantly to us was Saint Theresa of Lisieux, 'the Little Flower', the recent French saint after whom our parish and school were named and whose portrait hung in the school corridor. A tubercular Carmelite nun, Saint Theresa had died in 1897, aged twenty-four, and been canonised in 1925. Devotion to her, Patrick O'Farrell writes, 'was characterised by sweetness personified . . . passionate devotion to . . . small things done right for God . . . a tragic joyful paragon of virtue and prayer . . . Tough Irish spirituality, nurtured on combative aggressive saints . . . was drowned in the sea of international popular sentiment which welled up around this extraordinary obscure nun. Ordinary people, particularly women . . . identified with this strange transformation of obedience and submission and pain — and lack of human consequence — into love and joy and triumph over self. The ordinary Catholic world took her for their own.'[8]

Saint Theresa of Lisieux

Especially nuns. For nuns at this time carried much of the weight of parish responsibility, particularly in rural and provincial districts. At Saint Theresa's they taught, they gave religious instruction, they visited the sick, they acted as sacristans, they cleaned the church and school, they coached sport (basketball and rugby), they provided a congregation at Mass seven days a week, and — in the midst of all this — they tried to maintain a religious community life. And almost all of this was sustained financially on a small stipend from the parish and whatever Sister Domitille could earn from music lessons (and she was teaching piano to Catholic and non-Catholic pupils six days a week).

'Father', on the other hand — whether it was Father McGrath or Father Clancy or Father Kavanagh or Father Hyland — seemed to have an easier life. His meals were made for him, he had to do neither dishes nor housework, he was not tied daily to the classroom, he had a car in which he could travel — doing good works, of course, and sometimes dealing with people or relationships *in extremis*; but also recipient of endless morning and afternoon teas, and of considerable respect. Whenever any of these men came into the school for short periods to test our knowledge of the Catechism we would spend an hour tidying up the classroom and ourselves, the sisters would fuss around them with enormous solicitude, and at the end would say, 'Won't you give us your blessing, Father?' And we went down on our knees, eyes closed, and made the sign of the cross as Father dispensed more

Memorare

Remember, O most gracious Virgin Mary, that never was it known that anyone who fled to thy protection, implored thy help, and sought thy intercession, was left unaided. Inspired with this confidence, I fly unto thee, O Virgin of virgins, my Mother. To thee I come, before thee I stand, sinful and sorrowful. O Mother of the Word Incarnate, despise not my petitions, but in thy mercy, hear and answer me. Amen

grace in the Latin prescribed for such occasions. I knew even then what I would prefer to do: being a priest was a lot more fun than being a nun.

And here the devotion to Saint Theresa and the dedication of the school to her may have helped. To quote O'Farrell again, the Little Flower 'canonised pain and weariness, submission and oppression, frustration of the self'[9] and all these things would have been experienced far more by religious women at this time than by priests. The proximity of the Little Flower also helped to sanitise death. When Peter Darlington, a classmate, succumbed to leukaemia, the sisters told us he was 'with Saint Theresa' and that the saint especially loved children who died innocent and young. Our vision of this little boy, translated into Heaven with the morose Saint Theresa of the painting in the corridor, surrounded by the lachrymose angels who circled her in the picture, was a long way from the mundanities of the sick bed and the hospital ward.

The whole question of 'innocence' was one that puzzled and disturbed us. Another saint held up to us for veneration was Dominic Savio, a nineteenth-century Italian boy who was canonised while I was at school. His especial grace, Sister Isidore told us, was that he had died before 'maturity'. Hence he was entirely free from sins — or even temptations — of the flesh. What were these apparently unavoidable but unspecified sins that came with maturity? What exactly was 'the flesh' (for me this conjured up visions of Mr Casey the butcher slicing gleaming red eye-fillet for my mother)? We were left with a strong impression that it was better to die young and 'innocent' than it was to be polluted by the dreaded worlds of adolescence and adulthood.

So long as we did live, however, we were energetic believers in 'numerical Christianity and its calculator mentality'.[10] My mother, a former Child of Mary, had signed up with the Sodality of the Sacred Heart and the Association of the Perpetual Lamp. Both offered highly specific indulgences in return for spiritual duties (prayer to Our Lady of Mount Carmel, 100 days' indulgence; ejaculation to Our Lady of Mount Carmel, 300 days' indulgence; 'Saint Theresa intercede for us', thirty days' indulgence). Indulgences were reductions of time spent in Purgatory — though how 'time' was to be applied to the 'no-time' of eternity was a mystery to us.

We went to Mass on nine consecutive 'First Fridays' and five 'First Saturdays' to earn further remissions. We totted up 'plenary' indulgences by observing conditions attached to the Forty Hours' adoration of the Blessed Sacrament. For Mother's Day 1956 I gave my own mother a 'spiritual bouquet' of 'five Masses, five Communions, fourteen rosaries, twenty Stations of the Cross, five

Pugilist Father Frank Wall risks another bloodied nose, this time at Saint Peter Chanel School, Motueka. The nuns looking on, Sisters Patrice McGrath and Margaret Mary Dwane, belong to Mother Mary MacKillop's Sisters of Saint Joseph of the Sacred Heart ~ the 'Brown Joes'.
~ *Marist Archives*

Benedictions and seventy Hail Marys' — all offered up for her physical and spiritual well-being. For additional protection we resorted to the paraphernalia of talismans: a crucifix around the neck, wearing rosary beads, the Miraculous Medal, the Scapular — all of which (again) held out the possibility of specified remissions and indulgences. We did not go so far as Matt Talbot, the saintly Dubliner and reformed drunkard who, we were told, had worn chains around his body so tightly that the flesh had grown over them.

I was myself responsible for inflicting mortification on another saintly man. Father Frank Wall, a gnome-like figure exuding considerable energy, visited the school once a year to oversee the progress of Maori students (he was a Maori missioner), to tell stories to the whole school and to persuade the boys to go a round of manly boxing with him. I loved his stories, most of which were tear-jerkers about death-bed conversions or Maori children enduring illness heroically and exhibiting wisdom that confounded their elders. I did not like the boxing. The first occasion we squared up, boxing-gloved, he said, 'Hit me.' I said, 'No, Father, I can't.' He said, 'Go on, just try. I'll show you how to block.' I kept refusing and he kept encouraging me. Suddenly I lashed out straight through his guard. He took the full force of the blow on the nose and bled profusely. As Sister Isidore wiped his face and laid a cold compress over his nose she kept looking at me and shaking her head. 'I don't know, Father. I thought that boy would have been the last person to behave like a thug . . .'

Father Wall took us by bus to Pukekaraka, the Maori mission at Otaki founded by the French Marist Father Jean-Baptiste Comte in 1844. It was also the site of another school staffed by our Black Saint Josephs. First we looked at Rangiatea, the beautiful Anglican Maori church said to have been built with Te Rauparaha's blessing, and then at Father Comte's Saint Mary's, reputed to be the oldest Catholic church in the country. We had a talk on Maori history and culture outside the mission meeting house and made the Stations of the Cross up Pukekaraka Hill, like true pilgrims. It was a day full of interest and history, illuminated by the warmth of the Maori parishioners who entertained and fed us, and by Father Wall's jovial but no-nonsense manner. He is the only person I have ever hit deliberately — and probably the person I least wanted to hurt. When I last saw him at Pat Lawlor's funeral in 1979, he led a procession of priests that solemnly preceded the coffin. As he passed my pew he caught my eye, rubbed his nose and winked.

Saint Francis Xavier ~ Patron of Missions Patron of Australia and New Zealand

We knew the Lawlors because they had a bach at Plimmerton. Pat — a journalist, author and bookman — was especially kind to the family when I contracted polio because he too had had it as a child and consequently walked with a limp. When he was buried, however, it was from Saint Mary of the Angels in Wellington — the only Catholic church in the country whose arches and stained glass give one a hint of what it might be like to be in a European cathedral. In later years I came to value it for this atmosphere, and for the performance of sung Masses at Easter and Christmas by Maxwell Fernie's choir. My first view of it, however, was in May 1954, when my older sister, Louise, took me to see Thomas O'Shea lying in state.

Poor Archbishop O'Shea. He had had to wait more than twenty years as coadjutor bishop for his boss, Archbishop Redwood, to die. His own last years as a bishop were dogged with poor health. To a child, he was far more impressive in death than in life. He was a short man with a large forehead; his birettas and mitres always appeared too small for him and looked as if a breath of wind would knock them off. He seemed too to have retained the vestiges of an American accent (having been born in San Francisco in 1870) or an Irish one. When I heard him speak at a Confirmation service, he kept talking about 'car-licks', which baffled the children present. My mother explained afterwards that he meant 'Catholics'.

Opposite ~ Saint Mary of the Angels, Wellington, home for Maxwell Fernie's celestial music and the New Zealand church most like a European cathedral. ~ *Marist Archives*

In May 1954 the archbishop was laid out in his coffin in purple episcopal robes. His mitre seemed to fit at last. He looked peaceful and majestic, if paler and even shorter than before. Louise and I

SUB MARIÆ NOMINE.

Archbishop Thomas O'Shea in his prime and full regalia, including the pallium around his neck. Unlike those of his successors forty years later, ceremonial garments and accoutrements of this time lacked New Zealand elements.
~ Pat Lawlor Collection

joined a queue that shuffled up the centre aisle from the back of the church, around the coffin and out a side door. We were so impressed that we went back and did it a second time. Our non-Catholic friends were jealous. They had never seen anybody dead. There was no doubt about it, they told us: being Catholic was more interesting than being Protestant.

Apart from these sometimes exotic memories, what stayed with us as a consequence of growing up in this seamless and self-contained world of pre-Vatican II Catholicism?

Firstly and fundamentally, of course, we learned the tenets of our religion through instruction and recitation of the Catechism. God had made us; man (it was always 'man' at that time) had rejected God's love and grace by sinning in the Garden of Eden; Jesus Christ had become man to redeem us by His suffering and death on the cross; Heaven was now open to everybody who was baptised and accepted God's grace; the Catholic Church was the One True Church, founded by Jesus Christ and entrusted to Saint

Peter and his papal successors; we were obliged to marry Catholics and raise children as Catholics; we were not to attend Protestant services — whether baptisms, weddings, funerals or Anzac Day parades — unless we had a dispensation from our parish priest; we were forbidden to eat meat on Fridays.

Beyond the formal teaching about dogma and discipline, however, the ethics of Christianity were communicated through discussion of scripture, stories of the lives of saints and — most especially — through the living example of the sisters who taught us, our parents, our grandparents, our fellow parishioners such as Pat Lawlor — a man who was humble and prayerful in private life and gave radiant and sometimes controversial witness to Catholic principles in his public life as a writer.

I was fortunate to escape the spirit of Jansenism that pervaded pockets of Irish Catholicism in New Zealand. The Catholicism we encountered in Father McGrath's sermons was largely of a cheerful and positive kind, a religion that stressed the redeeming power of love more than punishment for trivial sins. 'For God did not send His Son into the world to condemn the world,' he thundered from the pulpit, 'but so that the world might be saved through Him.' And it would be saved through love: love of God for humanity, and of humanity for God and one another. The practical application of this formula stressed most often to me at home and at school was the one of doing unto others as you would have them do to you. I was taught that the most profound satisfaction came from service, from giving rather than taking. In the lives of our precious Sisters of Saint Joseph I saw daily evidence that this was so. And they reinforced the living message by teaching us the prayer of Saint Francis of Assisi:

'Where there is hatred, let me sow love; where there is injury, pardon; where there is doubt, faith; where there is despair, hope; where there is darkness, light; where there is sadness, joy . . . For it is in giving that we receive . . .'[11]

At home and school too we were heavily imbued with the parable of the talents. Each individual was born with an obligation to change the world for the better ('You are not here for good living,' Sister Isidore used to say, 'but to make living good'). And of those to whom much was given, much was expected. After despair, the greatest sin was that of refusing to recognise, to develop and to use God-given gifts. In addition to being a prescription for spiritual growth this was also the basis for an interventionist and optimistic approach to the problems of the world.

Out of these beliefs developed a conscience, a loud and active inner voice that regulated our behaviour. It served also to keep us honest. In the religious atmosphere of my childhood there

Prayer of Saint Francis

Lord, make me an
instrument of Your Peace.
Where there is hatred,
let me sow love;
Where there is injury,
pardon;
Where there is doubt, faith;
Where there is despair, hope;
Where there is darkness,
light;
Where there is sadness, joy.

O Divine Master, grant that
I may seek not so much to be
consoled as to console; to be
understood as to understand;
to be loved as to love. For it
is in giving that we receive;
it is in pardoning that we
are pardoned and it is in
dying that we are born to
Eternal Life.
Amen

With tens of thousands of New Zealand Catholics we attended Father Patrick Peyton's Rosary Crusade in the Marian Year of 1954. The motto he preached was 'the family that prays together stays together'. Also on the platform, Father John Curnow and Bishop Edward Joyce.
~ *Christchurch Diocese*

was no hair-splitting about the nature of Truth. Truth was, in the Thomistic phrase, the agreement of the mind with reality. Disagreement of the mind with reality — self-deception or telling lies — was a sin against both God and nature and troubled us greatly. It also made life more complicated. We came to place a high value on honesty — not simply as a moral imperative but as a condition necessary for peace of mind.

Catholicism's other enduring gift from this time was an awareness of the power of language and ritual, both of which connected us to our history and to our deepest race memories. The Latin Mass was a source of profound solemnity and joy. There were the embroidered vestments, the mannered movements, the mysterious manipulation of bread and wine, the consecration bells. At High Masses there was the addition of incense, chanting and singing. But, above all, and at all Masses, there were the words. The effect began with the sound of the spoken Latin, sonorous, oratorical and highly pleasing:

Credo in unum Deum,
Patrem omnipotentem,
factorem caeli et terrae,
visibilium omnium et invisibilium.[12]

Added to this was the meaning of the words, filtered to us through the slightly archaic idiom of the Douai Bible, which intensified the gravity and the beauty:

I will wash my hands among the innocent
and will encompass Thine altar, O Lord,
that I may hear the voice of praise
and tell of all Thy wondrous works.
I have loved, O Lord, the beauty of Thy house
and the place where Thy glory dwelleth.
Take not away my soul with the wicked
nor my life with men of blood,
in whose hands are iniquities,
their right hand is filled with gifts.
But as for me, I have walked in innocence.
Redeem me and have mercy on me.[13]

We basked in the knowledge that these words and the movements and gestures that accompanied them constituted a ritual hallowed by time and history. They had been practised unchanged for centuries. Our forefathers in England and Ireland had risked death to hear these sacred and radiant sounds. And this very same liturgy was being celebrated in precisely the same way, minute by minute, in almost every other country in the world. It was an umbilical cord that bound us to the past and penetrated national cultures. And it was, we believed, unchanging and unchangeable.

CHAPTER ONE

First Footprints

THE FIRST CATHOLICS known to have set foot on New Zealand soil did so in 1769.

The initial group were crew members on James Cook's barque HMS *Endeavour*, which put the first Europeans ashore in New Zealand at Poverty Bay on 8 October. Other landings were made along the east coast of the North Island between October and the end of that year. Although the bulk of the crew were English and nominally members of the Church of England, Catholics aboard *Endeavour* included a Cork Irishman named John Marra, two Italians, Antonio Ponto and John Baptista, and a Portuguese, Manoel Pereira, who had joined the ship at Rio and was punished by Cook for stealing kumara from Bay of Islands Maori in November 1769.[1]

Two months after that first landing, a vessel owned, captained and crewed by European Catholics passed within kilometres of *Endeavour* in a storm off North Cape. This was the appropriately named French merchantman *Saint Jean-Baptiste*, which came in sight of the west coast of the North Island on 12 December 1769 and anchored in Doubtless Bay on 17 December. Here the crew

Opposite ~ Maori Madonna and Child, carved for a Catholic chapel in the Bay of Plenty, 1840s.
~ *Auckland Institute & Museum*

went ashore and recorded observations of native New Zealanders over a fortnight. And on Christmas Day 1769 they participated in the first Christian service conducted in the country.[2] For the captain, Jean-François-Marie de Surville, was not only a devout practitioner of his religion: he brought with him a Dominican priest, Father Paul Antoine Leonard de Villefeix, as expedition chaplain.

It was, of course, part of the presumption of the envoys of eighteenth- and nineteenth-century European culture, including Surville and his chaplain and crew, to believe that Aotearoa New Zealand was without religion or civilisation until the arrival of Christians. Pottier L'Horme, Surville's company officer, described Doubtless Bay Maori as 'barbarians . . . lazy to the last degree, treacherous, thieving, defiant, and on the lookout to surprise you without thinking twice, which goes to show their limited intelligence'. He went on to say that, because of the Frenchmen's inability to communicate with Maori, 'I have been unable to ascertain with what kind of cult they know [their] god, nor whether they recognise several gods . . .'[3]

The very words applied to Maori by L'Horme and his contemporaries — cult, barbarians, savages, heathens — would have seemed to indicate to most Europeans that the writers were describing a people without enlightenment, without religious practices, without moral scruples. And when at last Catholic missionaries in the nineteenth century sought a Maori word for the gift of Faith which they had carried with them half-way round the globe, they settled upon Whakapono — 'the shedding of light or truth', as if only darkness had preceded them.

All this is understandable, coming as it did from the emissaries of cultures which believed that their technological superiority over indigenous peoples equated with spiritual and moral superiority; and that there was but one God who had revealed Himself in — successively — the Middle East, the Mediterranean, and then the nations of Northern and Western Europe. Since Pope Paul III's Bull of 1537 Catholics had been reminded that indigenous peoples were as much human beings as their colonisers and conquerors, and that they enjoyed the same natural rights. But this affirmation was accompanied by the belief that 'Indians' were nevertheless heathens and pagans — people requiring enlightenment in spiritual matters and God's grace for eternal salvation.

In New Zealand such a view may have obscured the fact that religion had permeated Maori life for a millennium before the arrival of Europeans — and Polynesian life for at least another millennium before migration to New Zealand. Maori had recognised atua or spiritual powers in Nature: in Tane Mahuta's offerings of food and shelter from the forests, in Tangaroa's gifts of fish and shellfish from the sea, even in the cleansing storms and winds of Tawhirimatea. There were also atua who resided in and protected particular geographical features and places.

Nothing was taken from the domain of these atua without respect, propitiation and expressions of gratitude. Maori religious beliefs — about atua, tupua, mana, tapu, noa and mauri — harmonised the workings of mind and body and spiritual realities with physical. The whole of existence was bound up in a unified vision in which each aspect of life was related to every other. These beliefs and the practices and rituals associated with them affected human behaviour from Te Rerenga Wairua in the north to Rakiura in the south.

All of which meant that Maori — so-called heathen — were far more receptive to consideration and discussion of religious issues, once bilingualism made such discussions possible, than were, say, the secularised humanists of the European Enlightenment and their successors. Maori believed already in atua; it did not require a large movement of faith to accept belief in a single God, Te Atua (indeed, there is evidence for a supreme deity, Io, in some Maori cosmologies). Maori already believed that tikanga or codes of behaviour regulated the workings of communities; it was not such a big transition to consider an alternative code, even if it did outlaw such aspects of tikanga Maori as eating human flesh or keeping slaves.

The major points of Christian belief that contrasted with tikanga Maori were the notions that natural man was a fallen creature needing to be redeemed by Christ's suffering and death; and that every human life — whether of rangatira, commoner or slave — was of equal value in the eyes of Te Atua and those who acknowledged Him.[4]

Such considerations lay well in the future for Maori who witnessed French Catholic seamen coming ashore at Rangiaohia in Doubtless Bay in December 1769. The visitors' only preparation for the encounter to follow was an inaccurate summary of Abel Tasman's journal, which described how the Dutchman had lost four crew members to attacking Maori in Golden Bay in 1642. To the surprise of the Frenchmen, however, Maori in Doubtless Bay made them welcome. '[They] were scattered here and there on the hills and the shore, and [did] honour to the new arrivals by waving things constantly to one side, as though to create a breeze . . . [Some] had long-haired skin cloaks, and others had bunches of grass.'[5]

Among those who went ashore and glimpsed Maori life at close quarters during the fortnight that the *Saint Jean-Baptiste* remained in Doubtless Bay was Father Leonard de Villefeix, Dominican priest and ship's chaplain. He was forty-one years of age, born

Ranginui of Te Patupo, kidnapped by Captain de Surville from Doubtless Bay in 1769. Speculation that he may have been the first Maori Christian is not well founded.
~ Archive General de Indias, Sevilla

near Etouars in Perigord in 1728. He came from an apparently good family and one of his brothers, Leonard de Lestang, became parish priest of Etouars.

Father Villefeix seems to have joined the *Saint Jean-Baptiste* expedition at the request of the Surville family, who were noted for their piety (one of Captain Surville's aunts had founded a religious community, and his mother had been referred to by the Bishop of Halicarnassus as 'the mother of missionaries').[6] There is no evidence that Father Villefeix attempted to proselytise among the Maori — although he did wander, unaccompanied by fellow crew members, through one of the villages on the Karikari Peninsula.

Whatever missionary zeal he or Surville may have had would have been blunted by the fact that in 1769 no Maori spoke French and no Frenchman spoke Maori. Had both parties been able to communicate, Father Villefeix might have made much of the fact that Rangiaohia, where the Frenchmen came ashore, had also been the landing place of the *Mamaru* canoe, which brought the ancestors of the local people to Doubtless Bay. And Rangiaohia was in addition said to be where humankind learned the art of netting from the Paiarehe or light-skinned fairy folk.[7] This tradition provided a metaphor which any Catholic priest, ordained to be, like Saint Peter, a fisher of men, would have found irresistible. So this could be considered an opportunity lost.

"Je crois a la vie éternelle ~ enfer"

Unquestionably, however, Father Villefeix was the first Christian minister to set foot on New Zealand, pre-dating the better-known Church Missionary Society priest Samuel Marsden by forty-four years; and he was the first ordained minister to lead a Christian service there, being required to say Mass on Sundays and holy days of obligation (of which Christmas Day 1769, when the *Saint Jean-Baptiste* was still in Doubtless Bay, was one). Regrettably, surviving journals of the voyage of the *Saint Jean-Baptiste* are silent on this point, though they record Father Villefeix leading prayers for the sick on board ship on Christmas Eve and for burials in Doubtless Bay. As Professor John Dunmore has pointed out, however: 'Priests were expected to say daily Mass, and required to say Sunday Mass, ditto for Christmas Day . . . Church services are not usually recorded in log book/journals any more than watch duties or the cook preparing a meal . . .'[8]

The Frenchmen abandoned the New Zealand coast on 31 December 1769 in some disillusionment after experiencing storms, the deaths of sick crew members and the theft of the ship's yawl. They had not made, nor apparently sought to make, Catholic converts among Maori. Given that other native peoples among the crew of the *Saint Jean-Baptiste* had been baptised, however, some have speculated that Ranginui, a Te Patupo chief kidnapped by Surville in retaliation for the theft, may have become the first Maori Christian. It seems unlikely. No mention of such a baptism survives in the ship's records. And although one of the ship's officers reported that Ranginui 'no longer seems sad [and] laughs with everybody', the hapless chief died of scurvy on 24 March 1770, in sight of the Juan Fernandez Islands off South America. It is doubtful that in three months he could have acquired sufficient fluency in French to be interested in, let alone instructed in, what would have been for him an alien faith.[9] Did Father

Villefeix none the less conduct last rites over Ranginui, believing that the genial New Zealander may have exhibited 'baptism of desire'? Again, we have no way of knowing.

Less than two weeks later Captain Surville too perished, drowned while trying to land through surf on a Peruvian beach. Seventeen months on, while the *Saint Jean-Baptiste* was being held by Spanish authorities in Callao, Surville's nephew and Father Villefeix jumped ship to go goldmining up an inland South American river.

Over the next two decades there were no Catholics in New Zealand other than when ships called with Catholics among the crews. Surville's compatriot Marc-Joseph Marion du Fresne brought two vessels around the Northland coast in April 1772, and put men ashore at Spirit's Bay and Tom Bowling Bay, and then in the Bay of Islands, where he and twenty-six of his crew were killed by Maori in June. An Italian named Alessandro Malaspina led a two-ship Spanish expedition into Doubtful Sound in February 1793; they stayed only two days, but as one of those days was Sunday and both vessels had chaplains, it is probable that once again Mass was celebrated in New Zealand waters.[10] Antoine Raymond Joseph Bruni d'Entrecasteaux paid an equally brief visit to Northland the following month as part of a voyage in search of the missing French navigator La Pérouse.

"Jugement particulier ~ du juste"

As the 1790s advanced towards the turn of the nineteenth century, however, temporary residents — many of them escaped convicts or former convicts from the Australian colonies — began to fetch up on the New Zealand coast. Forty sealers were landed on Anchor Island in Dusky Sound in 1792, for example. Other sealing gangs out of Port Jackson and Hobart worked subsequently around the Fiordland and Foveaux Strait coasts. In 1795, 244 passengers from New South Wales, forty-six of them escaped convicts, were stranded for nearly a year at Facile Harbour in Dusky Sound after the ship carrying them sank. The last of their party were not rescued until 1797. Towards the end of the decade members of visiting crews began to jump ship and live ashore in the Bay of Islands and the Hauraki Gulf, ports where vessels were calling in increasing numbers for timber and flax. Given the high proportion of Catholic Irish among the population of the Australian penal colonies, it is inevitable that some of these temporary settlers and Pakeha–Maori would have been Catholic. But their names are largely unknown.

It seems odd that there should have been Catholic clergy in Australia as early as 1800 but none — other than Father Villefeix

— in New Zealand until 1838. The reasons lie in the vicissitudes of European history. The Jesuits, who had borne most of the burden of the Church's 'foreign missions' in India, Asia and the Americas, and who had reached the Mariana Islands in the Pacific from the Philippines in the mid-seventeenth century, were withdrawn from such work in 1773 — just when the visits of Cook, Surville and du Fresne might have kindled European interest in New Zealand. Franciscans from Peru failed in an attempt to establish a mission in the Society Islands in 1774–75. In England, source of the colonisation of Australia and of so many ship visits to New Zealand in the late eighteenth and early nineteenth centuries, the practice of the Catholic Faith and hence its propagation was legislatively discouraged until the passing of the Catholic Emancipation Bill by Parliament in 1829. Roman Catholic dioceses with residential bishops were not re-established in England until 1850.

Even in Australia the earliest Catholic clergy were there only because they were convicts and they dispensed the sacraments without the formal approval of ecclesiastical or civil authorities. The first official Catholic chaplains were not permitted to work there until 1820. Samuel Marsden, the powerful Church of England chaplain who sent the first Protestant missionaries to New Zealand in 1814, opposed any toleration of Catholicism in New South Wales, stating that 'if Mass were allowed, the Colony would be lost to the British Empire in less than one year'. Further, he confessed himself to be haunted by 'a nightmarish fear of Irish barbarism'.[11] One can assume that he would have been just as opposed to the encouragement of Catholicism and Irish barbarism in New Zealand.

"Jugement particulier ~ du pécheur"

Father Villefeix's countrymen, who might have provided an alternative source for Catholic evangelisation (and did eventually) were prevented initially from doing so by the French Revolution and then by two decades of Anglo-French wars, which diverted resources and made it impossible for French vessels to provision and refit ships in British ports, such as those in Australia, between 1795 and 1815. Hence there were no further visits of French ships to New Zealand between d'Entrecasteaux's expedition in 1793 and Louis-Isidore Duperrey's in 1824.

Appropriately enough, though, when the Catholic Church did begin to give methodical consideration to the conversion of the 'savages' of the South Pacific, it was as a consequence of an Irish-French initiative.

Peter Dillon, the ship's captain who had taken Marsden's first Church Missionary Society workers to New Zealand in 1814, was a six-foot-four-inch red-headed Catholic Irishman born in Martinique in 1788. In twenty years of sailing and trading in the

Pacific he came to know its islands and their inhabitants more intimately than any other seaman of his time. Eventually he became indignant that his own religion was not available either to indigenous islanders or expatriate Europeans in the region. This sense of indignation increased as he saw Protestant missionaries — Anglicans and Wesleyans — begin to make inroads among island populations, including the Maori in New Zealand.

By this time there was one Catholic mission in the Pacific. The French order of the Congregation of the Sacred Hearts of Jesus and Mary — known as the Picpus Fathers after the street in Paris where their mother house stood — had begun to preach in Hawaii in 1825. They were expelled from there by the Polynesian queen of the islands and, subsequently, readmitted. From 1833 Picpus priests were given responsibility for evangelising the Marquesas, Tuamotus and Society Islands, the area subsequently known as French Polynesia. But these arrangements did not include the islands of the west and south Pacific.

In 1829 Peter Dillon was in France to receive civic honours for his role in solving the mystery of what had happened to the La Pérouse expedition, which had disappeared after its two ships left Botany Bay in 1788. Dillon met and had long conversations with the Reverend Patrick McSweeny, Rector of the Irish College in Paris (which, because of anti-Catholic laws in Britain, had been established to train clergy for Ireland). McSweeny shared Dillon's enthusiasm for the prospect of a South Pacific mission and introduced the ship's captain to Father Gabriel Henri Jerome de Solages, a wealthy but sickly aristocrat, who was Prefect of Bourbon (Reunion Island) in the Indian Ocean.[12]

As a result of their collaborations, Solages was later that year appointed Prefect Apostolic of the South Seas, making him responsible for Catholic evangelisation over sixty-five million square miles covering islands south of the equator, from New Zealand in the west to Easter Island in the east. It was, in effect, the largest diocese in the world. The document confirming this appointment, dated 16 January 1830, is the first originating from the Vatican to specifically recognise New Zealand as part of an ecclesiastical territory.[13]

Solages also had the backing of the French Government. The next stage of the plan was to have been a round-the-world voyage by a French Navy supply ship which, after visiting French bases in South America, would land French missionaries and stores at Pitcairn, Tonga, Samoa, Fiji and New Zealand. It was expected that Peter Dillon would captain the vessel. Just when all was ready to proceed, there was a political change of seismic proportions. The July Revolution in Paris swept away the restored monarchy, the government and senior civil servants. The navy withdrew its support for the plan and it collapsed. And Father Solages, although nominally in ecclesiastical authority over the South Pacific, was unable to visit the region before he died in Madagascar in 1832.

There was one valuable precedent in all of this, however. Rome had opened the Pacific as a specifically French mission and identified New Zealand as part of it. And when the western part of the region was designated the Vicarate of Western Oceania in 1835, a French bishop and French priests and religious were charged with staffing it.

❖

Meantime, independent of this ecclesiastical bureaucratic activity, New Zealand had continued to attract a growing but still priestless Catholic population. In the 1820s and 1830s further Irish settlers migrated from Australia to the Hokianga, the Kaipara, the Bay of Islands, the Firth of Thames and the Bay of Plenty. In the latter decade they were joined by a smaller number of French settlers. And it was these men and women, along with a handful of Maori adherents, who established the Catholic Church in New Zealand and gave it a permanent presence. Where was that Church? asked historian Ernest Simmons. '[Among] the shifting population of hundreds of seamen, logging camps, timber workers, traders and merchants . . .'[14]

Most of these men — and they were almost without exception men — were what Simmons identified as 'the ordinary men of the New Zealand of their day . . . [They were] regarded by the Protestant missionaries as pagans, given to drink and fornication, men who enjoyed living in one of the toughest places in the world. As time went on most of them settled down to married life . . . But even then their lives seldom followed the pattern of civilised respectability. The point is . . . that they were Catholics, that they remained Catholics, and that they made some efforts to make their Catholic faith known to the Maoris.'[15] This last comment was true especially of those who, like Thomas Cassidy of Waima in the Hokianga, lived with and subsequently married Maori women.

What kind of Church was it? These early Catholic migrants, like others, brought with them 'the spiritual and intellectual baggage already acquired . . . Irish Catholicism before the Famine years was a bewildering mixture of formal Catholicism, debased Catholic practices, family piety, superstition, magic and Celtic mythology . . . [It was] a poem that gave life meaning or respite. It was a view of the world enabling one to sustain the present and hope for the future. It was also a folk culture, a bond of loyalty to one's fellows.'[16]

Thomas and Mary Poynton, the mother and father of Catholicism in New Zealand, in old age.
~ Marist Archives

The best-known of these early New Zealand-Irish Catholics, and by far the most respectable, was a stocky and doggedly determined trader named Thomas Poynton. He had been born in County Meath in 1803. After receiving part of his education in France, Poynton had by 1822 been transported to New South Wales for a political offence.[17] In 1828, having earned a reputation for reliability and clean living among the Irish community in Sydney, he married Mary Kennedy (Australian born but of Irish parentage). That same year they moved to the Hokianga Harbour on New Zealand's north-west coast, where Thomas established a store and sawing station.

The Poyntons did well at Totara Point on the Mangamuka River, largely because they maintained excellent relations with their Maori neighbours on the northern side of the harbour. Within a few years they owned their business and made a comfortable living. Thomas had taken upon himself the role of spokesman for New Zealand Catholics. Mary was of that stature and piety that attracted the epithet 'little Irish mother'. When the first two of their children were born she made the 1000-mile journey to Sydney to have them baptised.

In 1835 Thomas learned that a Benedictine from a German-English Catholic family, John Bede Polding, had been appointed Australia's first Catholic bishop, with responsibility for eight priests and 20,000 souls. He sailed again for Sydney and begged Polding to send a priest to New Zealand. The bishop was unable to do so: he had insufficient clergy for his own far larger flock, and New Zealand was not part of his sphere of responsibility. Polding was clearly touched by Poynton's appeal, however, and sent the pious Irishman home with books of religious education and prayer, and with highly specific instructions:

'His Lordship authorised me to warn Catholics that none of them were to attend any of the Protestant preachers in Hokianga, or elsewhere [up to this time, in what may have been an early but lukewarm spirit of ecumenism, some Hokianga Catholics living with Maori had been attending services with the Wesleyans]; furthermore his Lordship commanded me to visit those Catholics who were living with native women & that I was to get a promise from each of them that if ever a Catholic Priest arrived in New Zealand, they should marry these women & get them Baptised

Saintly English Benedictine John Bede Polding, first bishop to send a pastoral letter to Catholics in New Zealand.
~ *Auckland Diocese*

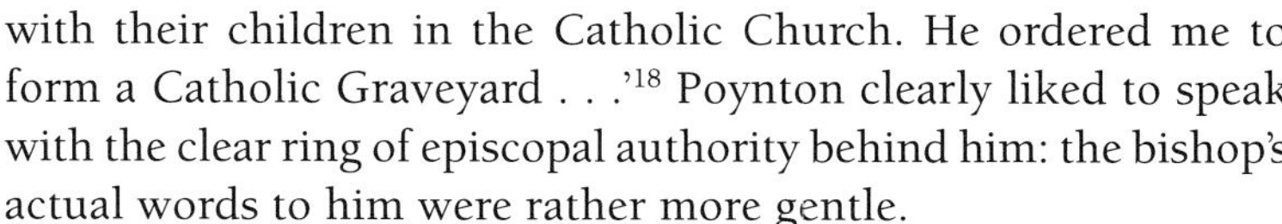

with their children in the Catholic Church. He ordered me to form a Catholic Graveyard . . .'[18] Poynton clearly liked to speak with the clear ring of episcopal authority behind him: the bishop's actual words to him were rather more gentle.

Back in the Hokianga Poynton gathered around him as many Catholics who could and would come to his home on Sundays, where Thomas now read aloud the prayers of the Mass and gave edifying instruction from the books which Bishop Polding had given him. In addition the family gathered every evening to recite the rosary and some Maori and Pakeha neighbours formed the habit of joining them.[19]

Hail Mary, full of grace,
the Lord is with thee.
Blessed art thou among
women, and blessed is the
fruit of thy womb, Jesus.
Holy Mary, Mother of God,
pray for us sinners, now
and at the hour
of our death.
Amen

That same year, in October 1835, another Hokianga Irish trader, Thomas Cassidy of Waima, took his partner Maraea Kuri to Sydney so that they might marry in Saint Mary's Cathedral and that Maraea and their first child might be baptised. And still another Irishman, name unknown, brought a young Maori man and woman to Sydney for presentation to Bishop Polding. 'Their relations, who were tribal chiefs, had sent them under the care of an Irish sailor, to have them instructed in the Catholic religion,' wrote Dr Ullathorne, Australian Vicar General. 'They were instructed and baptised and returned to their country. The latest news [is] that the new Christians, back with their tribe, have aroused the most lively interest there. Their reports have decided another chief to send a messenger to the bishop to express his own desire and that of his son to be instructed and baptised . . .'[20]

There were other Irish Catholics in the Far North of New Zealand in the mid to late 1830s. John Hayes had arrived in New Zealand in 1822 with his brother Thomas (who subsequently drowned). Jacky Marmon, an ex-convict, may have settled in the Hokianga as early as 1823 and been the first Catholic among permanent residents there (and one of those condemned by the Protestant missionaries for persistent drinking and fornication). A man named Murphy was subsequently married to his partner, Ihapera Mahima. William Flynn settled in the Hokianga with his family in 1837. Maurice Kelly lived initially on the Kaipara Harbour. And a Thomas Davies married a Martha Kelly. There was an Italian in Whangaroa, Dominique Ferraris; and in the Bay of Islands three Duvauchelle brothers (who moved subsequently to Akaroa), along with the Cafler and Bernard brothers, Pierre Bonnetin, Pierre Charles Potier and François Rozier.

The number of French Catholics in coastal settlements was rising in the late 1830s as French whalers began to use New Zealand ports. In 1838 fourteen French whaling ships passed through the Bay of Islands and fourteen were working off Banks Peninsula the same year. And it was purchase of land on Banks Peninsula by the whaler Jean François Langlois that led to the

Father Jean-Claude Colin of Lyon, first Superior of the Society of Mary, whose priests and brothers staffed the early Catholic mission in New Zealand.
~ *Marist Archives*

establishment of the French colony at Akaroa in 1840.

By 1838 Thomas Poynton estimated that there were forty to fifty Catholics in the Hokianga alone. And it was his relentlessly optimistic reports of the practice of Catholicism in New Zealand that led the Australian Vicar General to the conclusion that the time was 'very propitious for sending missionaries to [that] country'.[21] And come they did, that same year. But they were not Poynton's English clerical friends from Australia, nor fellow Irishmen; they were Frenchmen from Lyon, a consequence of that much earlier Gallic interest in evangelising the South Seas which had been given momentum nine years earlier by Peter Dillon and Father Solages.

After Gabriel Henri Jerome de Solages had died in Madagascar in 1832, his ambition to see the people of the Pacific converted to Catholicism was not forgotten. In 1833, when the Holy See divided his vast vicarate into Eastern and Western Oceania, the eastern section was given to the Picpus Fathers. Two and a half years later the western section was entrusted to a young French bishop, Jean-Baptiste François Pompallier, and a newly formed religious congregation in Lyon, the Society of Mary. The latter was based — as its name suggests — on the spirit and example of the Mother of Christ (its inspiration was the Mary of the Acts of the Apostles, waiting in constant faith-filled prayer with the Apostles in the Cenacle for the outpouring of the Spirit at Pentecost[22]). The venture was to be funded by the Society for the Propagation of the Faith, founded by a group of Lyonnais businessmen in 1822, which hoped to build up as large a role in the Catholic foreign missions as that assumed previously by the Jesuits. The territory covered by the new mission included New Guinea, the Marshall Islands, Tonga, Samoa, Wallis, Futuna and New Zealand.

Pierre Chanel ~ Saint Peter Chanel First martyr of Oceania

The pioneer missionary band made up of the bishop, four priests and three brothers, sailed from Le Havre on Christmas Eve 1836. Taking whatever vessels were available for each leg of the voyage it took them more than a year to reach New Zealand. *En route* they began to learn English. One priest died at sea. Two others and two brothers were landed on the Polynesian islands of Wallis and Futuna (one of these priests, Pierre Chanel, was killed on Futuna in 1841). In Tahiti, Pompallier baptised his first New Zealander (a young Maori boy whose French father was a ship's officer). It was there too that he made the decision to base his Oceanic mission in New Zealand. Soon afterwards he learned from Bishop Polding that Thomas Poynton had offered the Catholic Church land on the Hokianga Harbour.

The day for which Thomas and Mary Poynton and their co-religionists had been hoping and praying for the best part of a decade came on 10 January 1838. On a clear morning the schooner *Raiatea*, twelve days out of Sydney, sailed inside the high-duned northern head of Hokianga Harbour and up the 'river', as the locals called the vast waterway. Unbeknown to Pompallier, the arrival was highly auspicious in Maori eyes. The full name of the harbour was Te Hokianga-nui-a-Kupe, the great returning place of Kupe, traditionally the first Polynesian navigator to sight it; and the homeland from which he had come was Rangiatea — or, in Tahitian, Raiatea. The link between the two places was commemorated in the Maori proverb, 'E kore koe e ngaro, i ruia mai i Raiatea — For I shall not perish, but as a seed sent forth from Raiatea I shall flourish.'[23] The Pikopo (bishop) and his men, then, came literally in the path of Kupe to the returning place of

Jean-Baptiste Pompallier, the young and charismatic Vicar of Oceania who became New Zealand's first bishop.
~ *Auckland Diocese*

Kupe, as seeds sent forth from Raiatea. Poynton's Maori friends made much of this connection as they welcomed the missionaries ashore at Totara Point.[24]

Jean-Baptiste Pompallier (again, an auspicious name when its significance was explained to Maori) was at this time 'a handsome man of 36, tall, dark-haired, of brown complexion with hazel eyes. He came of a well-to-do commercial family in Lyon and, although he possessed no personal wealth, he had the manner, education and courtesy of a gentleman. He believed himself to be of aristocratic lineage . . . and expressed this belief in the dignity of his bearing . . . His expression [was] benevolent and he seems to have had more than his fair share of personal charm. Father Catherin Servant was seven years younger. He was to show himself a very good missionary . . . and an intelligent observer of native ideas and customs. Brother Michel, born Antoine Colombon . . . left the mission and the [Marists] within a couple of years.'[25]

Thomas Poynton, by virtue of the resources at his disposal and the fact that Bishop Polding had commended him to

Essential missionary equipment ~ Bishop Pompallier's travelling altar, on which he celebrated his first Mass in New Zealand in January 1838. Along with his regalia, the altar excited the interest and admiration of Maori congregations. It folded into a box the size of a suitcase.
~ Auckland Diocese

New Zealand's first Marist priest, Father Catherin Servant, arrived with Pompallier in January 1838. For most of his four years in New Zealand he lived at Purakau on Hokianga Harbour, where he wrote a book published 130 years later as *Customs and Habits of the New Zealanders 1838–42*.
~ *Marist Archives*

Pompallier, took charge of the Frenchmen. He lent his four-roomed cottage to the missionaries, who turned the main room into a chapel. The Poyntons meanwhile moved into their store until a permanent mission station could be built on six acres at Papakawau on the southern side of the harbour, which Poynton subsequently sold to Pompallier. This would not be ready until June 1838. Meanwhile the bishop's first Mass in New Zealand was celebrated in the Poynton's converted living-room on 13 January with as many Hokianga Catholics as possible participating inside the house and outside through the windows. This was followed by the first baptism performed by a Catholic priest: that of the Poyntons' baby daughter, Catherine. When their son, Edward, died unexpectedly a week later, he became the first Catholic in the country to receive a Church burial. Throughout this first week and beyond, Thomas, being trilingual, was instructing all three missionaries in English and Maori.

The Poyntons' taking on — and indeed taking over — the Catholic mission may have been essential for its early survival. Not long after their arrival the Frenchmen were challenged by southern Hokianga Maori who had been stirred into aggression by the Wesleyan missionary Nathaniel Turner. Turner not only believed that the French priests would be anti-British: he viewed the Catholic Church, with which he had had no previous contact, as the 'Great Whore of Babylon'.[26] He sent Wesleyan Maori to Totara Point to throw the Frenchmen and their belongings into the sea. What saved the missionaries from such a sacking was the fact that northern Hokianga Maori ranged themselves unanimously in support of Thomas Poynton and Pompallier — a fruit of the relationship of mutual trust and respect which the Poyntons had built up with their neighbours over a decade. Pompallier was greatly moved to hear his Maori neighbours tell the Wesleyans that an attack on the mission would be tantamount to an attack on Te Rarawa people of north Hokianga. In the face of this protective shield, the Wesleyan Maori withdrew and no further incidents of this kind occurred.

The fact that the mission's earliest activities seemed centred largely around the Poyntons and the Hokianga Irish community pointed up a difficulty that would eventually become a source of personal and institutional stress. The whole missionary enterprise had been founded and financed with the object of converting the indigenous peoples of the Pacific. As the Pakeha population in New Zealand was to grow, however, especially once organised European settlement of the country began in the 1840s, the Catholics among the colonists would expect their Church to make provision for them as a matter of first priority.

Another source of difficulty would become apparent in the appearance and character of Pompallier himself. He was a 'commanding figure in long purple soutane and sash, episcopal ring and great tasselled hat', eloquent in preaching once he had mastered the new languages, intelligent and charming in conversation.[27] Maori, who had never before seen a bishop of any denomination (the first resident Anglican bishop, George Augustus Selwyn, would not arrive in New Zealand until 1842), were transfixed by his manners and appearance and fascinated by his celibacy — another feature which distinguished Catholic priests from Protestants and gave them a tactical advantage: being free from family responsibilities they were able to travel unencumbered and live in Maori villages; they did not need to acquire forests or farms to support wives and children.

Because of Pompallier's striking leadership of the mission, Maori soon coined the name Pikopo (from the Latin episcopus: bishop) to describe Catholic converts among their people.

Protestant Maori, by contrast, were labelled Mihinare (for missionary). Many Maori in Northland showed a keen and early disposition towards Catholicism because they were engaged by the robes and the ritual long before they began to learn or to think about Catholic doctrine. And they were further impressed by portents, such as those apparently represented by the bishop's Christian name and the name of the vessel which had brought him to New Zealand. Later in the nineteenth century the term Katorika (Catholic) began to replace Pikopo in Maori usage.

Like most of the early French missionaries, Pompallier had no organisational skills or managerial experience. Appointed bishop at the unusually young age of thirty-four specifically for the Oceania mission, his great strengths were his dedication, his eloquence and his charm. His fault, however, was that his vision exceeded his resources. In the eyes of most of his priests, he tended to spend money recklessly when he had it; and sometimes when he did not have it. When the coffers were bare his response was to tell his missionaries that God or the Society for the Propagation of the Faith would provide. Sometimes they did; sometimes not. For this failing, and for his imperiousness with subordinates, Pompallier would gradually lose the trust of many of his priests and religious and his ecclesiastical career in New Zealand would end in disappointment and financial disaster.

In 1838, however, the origins of the New Zealand mission seemed redolent only of promise. After three months Pompallier and Father Servant were able to preach in Maori. And on 29 June 1838 the bishop said Mass at Papakawau and preached in Maori and English, regarding the occasion as confirmation that the Catholic Church was now implanted in New Zealand. Proselytising among the Maori quickly settled on a form which seemed spectacularly successful. Pompallier or Servant would open a meeting with a hymn and a prayer (the bishop was composing Maori hymns from the time he could speak the language). Then priest or bishop would preach to instruct. And then one of the Maori catechists would take over to debate doctrine with the Maori audience in Maori. One of these, an early Hokianga Catholic named Werahiko, was 'endowed with the imaginative and fiery eloquence which pleases the natives so much . . . he rarely failed to rouse the audience'.[28] Among the first Maori converts were this Werahiko (Francis) of Whirinaki, who had previously been known as Papahia; a Whirinaki chief named Tiro who took the baptismal name of Herehorio (Gregory); and Te Huhu from Pawarenga. The full record of the earliest Hokianga baptisms is lost, however, destroyed in the Rawene presbytery fire of 1932.

In May 1838 Pompallier reported to the Marist superior, Father Jean-Claude Colin, that the new headquarters at Papakawau was

He Kororia ki a Maria

Mo Maria aianei
O tatou waiata!
Kia kaha ra tatou,
Kia nui te aroha.

Tena hoki nga ahere
E wakahonore ana
Ki to ratou rangatira,
Ki a Maria ano ra.

Me kaperiere hoki,
I unga e te Atua,
Ka heke ki Nahareta,
Ka puta ki a Maria

Hymn by Bishop Pompallier

taking shape. 'There will be a reception room where a small number of the faithful will be able to hear Mass and receive the sacraments until a wooden chapel or church is built . . . [There] are three more rooms or rather three closets where we can each sleep and work. There it all is, the episcopal palace. Brother Michel will cook outside in a kind of closed shed as well he can, but cooking here is not difficult — potatoes, fish and pork for food and water to drink, are the diet of New Zealand.'[29]

That same month Pompallier visited the Bay of Islands and said Mass before 300 people — sailors and Maori and Pakeha local inhabitants — on board the French warship *Heroine* (which soon afterwards sailed to the Chatham Islands and bombarded Maori villages there in retaliation for the disappearance of a French whaling ship). In October 1838 the bishop went to Mangakahia in the Kaipara district at the request of the local chief Te Tirarau and an Irish sawyer living there with a Maori wife and children. Soon after came an invitation from the people of Mangonui on the north-east coast — close to where Surville had anchored in 1769 — who now said that they too wished to become Catholics. Pompallier reported to Rome on 10 November 1838 that he had baptised forty-four Maori in ten months, most of them chiefs, together with their wives and children. He added that five to six thousand more had indicated that they wanted baptism.

"L'âme en état de péché mortel"

While the projected figure is certainly suspect, Pompallier and Servant had every reason to believe that their mission had begun well. So did the Anglicans and Wesleyans. When the Frenchmen arrived in the Hokianga the Protestant missions had been operating in New Zealand for twenty-four years: the Church Missionary Society since Peter Dillon had taken its first workers to the Bay of Islands in 1814; and Wesleyans since 1822. The Anglicans were the more widespread, with a dozen stations in the far north (largely on the east coast), Waikato and Bay of Plenty. The Wesleyans were established mainly on the west coast of the North Island, including at Mangungu on the southern shore of Hokianga Harbour. Neither Church attracted a significant number of Maori converts until the late 1820s. And when numbers began to rise they almost certainly did so in response to the degree of dislocation occurring in Maori life at that time (defeats for the northern tribes in musket warfare, deaths of prominent chiefs, the impact of alcohol and disease on Maori communities in the North).

Opposite ~ Bishop Pompallier's 'Tree of the Church', with which his missionaries sought to explain to Maori the concept of Apostolic succession ~ the passing of authority from Christ, through the Apostles, through the Popes, through bishops and down to contemporary Catholic clergy. The Protestant Churches were represented as branches which had withered and broken off the main trunk.
~ *Auckland Diocese*

Both Protestant missions had established what they considered to be their spheres of influence and they were not pleased at the prospect of having to compete with 'Papists' for Maori souls — and French Papists at that. William Williams, one of the CMS missionaries at Paihia, wrote of Pompallier in 1839 as a 'shrewd,

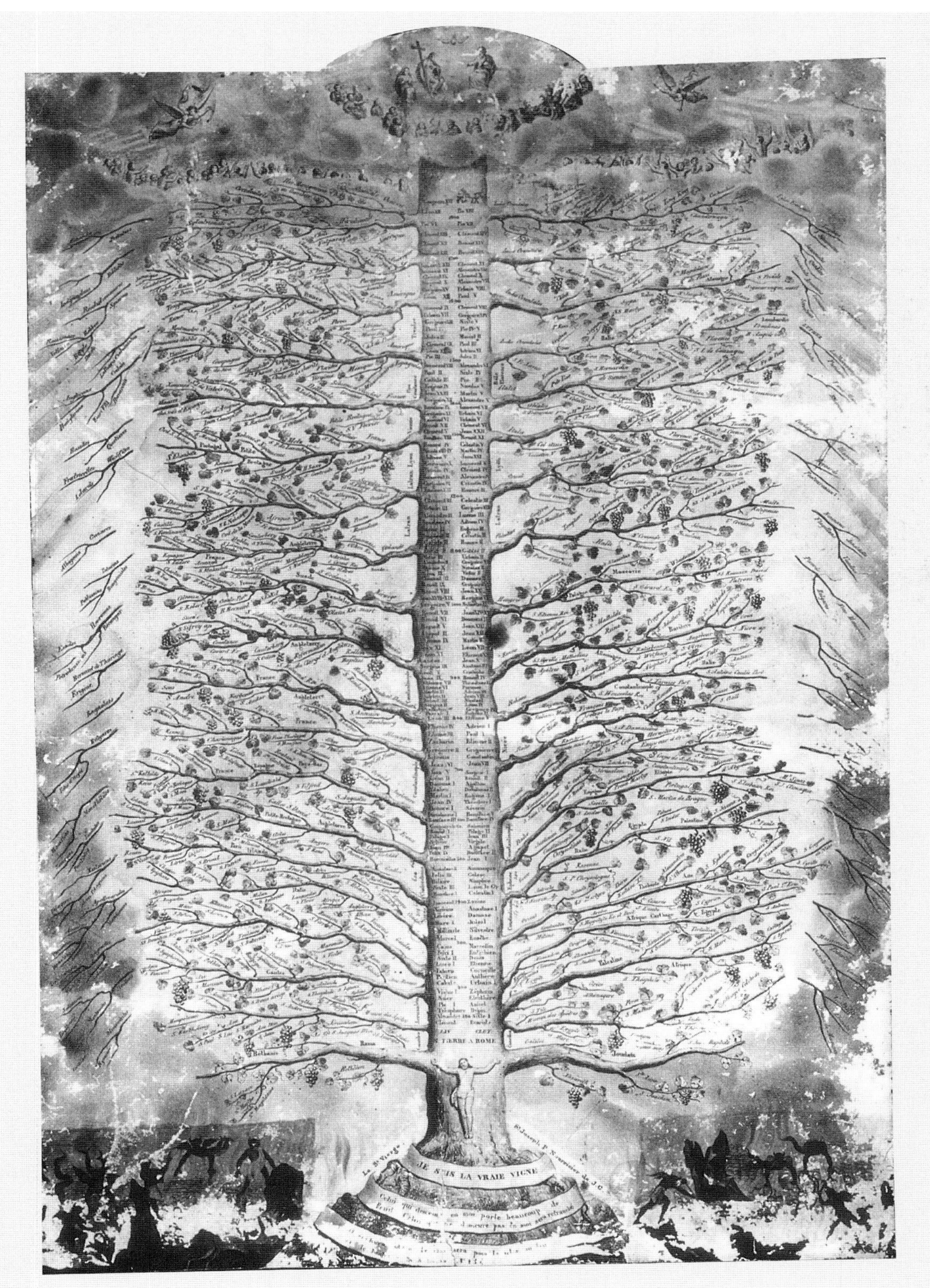

clever active man who is hindered by no difficulties and who hesitates not in the use of any means, whether lying or the employment of profligate Europeans in order to accomplish his purpose'.[30]

Relations between the Churches were complicated by the unfamiliarity of English Protestants with both the proximity and appearance of Catholic clergy (most had left England before the repeal of the penal laws), by traditional Anglo-French rivalry, and by a belief on the part of some British settlers in the Bay of Islands that France intended to colonise New Zealand and that the Catholic mission was an advance guard for this object. It should be noted too, however, that Catholics at this time were scarcely less tolerant of the Protestant missionaries: Thomas Poynton referred to his Wesleyan neighbours as 'mangy curs'; and Pompallier and Servant, while not personally abusive, certainly regarded Protestantism as 'a heresy to be refuted'.[31]

❖

In June 1839 the first of six bands of reinforcements arrived from France: Fathers Claude-André Baty, Maxime Petit and Jean-Baptiste Epalle, and Brothers Elie Régis, Augustin and Florentin. Pompallier crossed the hills to the Bay of Islands to welcome them. While there he bought a beachfront section and house at Kororareka to serve as new headquarters for the New Zealand and Oceanic mission. He had noted by this time that far more ships called in at the bay than anchored in the Hokianga, that the east coast of the North Island was more navigable than the west and had more ports, and that, with a British Resident at Waitangi, the Bay of Islands was developing into the nearest thing the country had to an administrative centre; indeed, when New Zealand was annexed by Britain the following year, the bay briefly became the site of the colony's first capital.

In February 1840 Pompallier was present at the meeting that led to the first signing of the Treaty of Waitangi, in which Maori leaders gave their consent to annexation by the British Crown. Although he expressed no view about the desirability of Maori giving up their sovereignty, the bishop did extract from the colony's first Governor, William Hobson, an assurance that the new administration would respect religious freedom (given that three denominations were already operating in New Zealand it made no sense to nominate one as an 'established Church', as in the United Kingdom). Subsequently, to emphasise their commitment to their country of adoption, Pompallier and some of his priests took British citizenship.

The accusation by some Protestants that members of the

Catholic mission were subversive because of their French origins was one that Pompallier and his priests sought to counter at every opportunity by stressing the international character of their Church. One such occasion occurred the same year as the treaty signing, when Bishop Polding and Dr Ullathorne — both English — arrived from Sydney for a short visit. They reported that they were 'received with joy' by the Marists at the Kororareka station.

'[The] residence was of wood, and their little wooden church, bright with green paint, stood adjoining; small as it was it had its font, confessional, and all appointments complete.' At evening devotions, 'one Father read the prayers before the altar in the native language, which the people answered, and then another Father intoned the hymn, which the people took up. It was the O Filii et Filiae, adapted to the New Zealand language, but in the old simple notes. How they did sing! . . . After this earnest act of devotion the senior missioner [Father Petitjean] addressed them. We could not understand what he said, but he every now and then pointed to us, and we heard the word "picopo".'[32]

The following year a large printery and storeroom, constructed Lyonnais-style with pressed earth walls, was added to the

Kororareka in 1843. The cluster of Catholic mission buildings is at top right, including (far right) Pompallier's house and next to it the first chapel. The printing house, the only one to survive, stands behind the other structures.
~ *Auckland Diocese*

The first sizeable Catholic church in New Zealand, built in wood at Kororareka in 1843. It burned down in 1896.
~ Auckland Diocese

Kororareka mission; and, behind that, a tannery. Then a new and larger church was built. The printing house accommodated a press which arrived from France in 1841 with a lay printer to operate it. Soon the mission was able to produce prayers, hymns and sections of the New Testament in Maori. The printery was the last mission building to survive in Kororareka, known later as Russell, and the one which, in the twentieth century, came to be called Pompallier House.

Meanwhile the Hokianga had not been abandoned. An important station was retained there, though late in 1839 its location was moved from Papakawau to Purakau (meaning, appropriately enough, 'the roots of the tree') on the northern side of the harbour. Here the Marists built a house and a tidal mill, and established a vineyard to produce table and altar wine. It remained the centre of Catholic Hokianga and of evangelising in the north of the country for much of the next seventy-five years. Initially, however, there was no church because there was no Maori community there. It became, in effect, a home base for the missionaries from which their work was done by visitation, by boat and on horseback, to the neighbouring villages and tribes. It was here that Father Servant began to write a perceptive and useful book on Maori customs and habits in October 1839.[33]

Troops continued to arrive from France as reinforcements for what the bishop termed 'God's army'. The December 1839 contingent was made up of Father Philippe Viard (who would in time become Pompallier's deputy and New Zealand's second bishop), Fathers Petitjean, Comte and Chevron, and Brother Attale. By 1840 the entire force was distributed thus: Father Epalle and Brother Elie at Whangaroa; Father Petitjean in charge at Kororareka; Fathers Servant, Baty and Comte at Purakau; Father Petit was responsible for the Kaipara mission; and Father Chevron and Brother Attale were sent north to Tonga. Father Viard, Brother

Father Jean-Baptiste Petitjean, pioneer Marist missionary.
~ *Marist Archives*

Father Jean-Baptiste Comte, first Marist Maori missionary in the Wellington district.
~ *Marist Archives*

Michel and a catechist named Romano sailed south with Pompallier in March 1840. They visited Otumoetai, Tauranga, Matamata, Opotiki and Whakatane, and Father Viard and Brother Michel were left at Tauranga to open a new station for the Bay of Plenty.

Back in Kororareka and anxious to find a cheaper way of servicing his entire western Pacific diocese the bishop bought a schooner, which he named *Sancta Maria*. In his first trip under his own sail, beginning in September 1840, Pompallier visited the new French colony at Akaroa (to which he had already sent Father Comte and a newly arrived colleague, Father Pezant, who thus became the first Catholic priests in the South Island). From Banks Peninsula the bishop went south to Otago, then north to Port Nicholson and the Mahia Peninsula. He said Mass for the first time in each district, and promised to send priests when he had sufficient resources to minister to the small Catholic populations there.

In July of the following year, after the arrival of still more priests (Fathers Garin, Borjon, Séon and Rozet), two candidates for the priesthood and five more brothers, Pompallier sailed south again in the *Sancta Maria*. He called at the country's new capital, Auckland, and celebrated Mass there for as many as 200 Irish Catholics. He then visited Coromandel, the Waikato, the Bay of Plenty (including a walk inland to Rotorua) and, again, Akaroa. He left priests at Matamata, Maketu, Opotiki and Mahia. At this point he was notified that his priest on Futuna, Pierre Chanel, had been killed, and he set sail for the Islands to recover the body and repair the mission there (the remains of Father Chanel, who was canonised in 1954, were kept at Kororareka until 1849, then Auckland, then France; they were returned to Futuna in the 1970s).

Pierre Chanel ~
Saint Peter Chanel

In the wake of his lengthy visits to the southern parts of the country, Pompallier felt that he had at last made progress in opening up the rest of New Zealand to missionary activities. By September 1841 he was able to list twelve stations there and three in Island Polynesia. At the same time he was now fully aware of the geographical area for which he was responsible, and of the immense difficulties involved in inland travel. The organised British colonisation of New Zealand had commenced in Auckland, Wellington, New Plymouth, Wanganui and Nelson, and would soon spread to Canterbury and Otago. This growth in the Pakeha population — which would inevitably include English and Irish Catholics — would require a huge increase in money and man-power to allow the mission to develop at the same rate as the nation as a whole. 'The Bishop's joy was overwhelming,' Father Garin reported when he landed in New Zealand in 1841. '[But] he told us that it would take fourteen times fourteen missionaries every six months for six years, and this would not be too many for the work in hand.'*[34]

In fact the bishop would never receive what he would consider to be adequate resources from the Society for the Propagation of the Faith to service even the Maori pastorate. This was apparent by 1842 when, in the course of Pompallier's visit to the Islands, the mission's financial affairs reached a crisis in New Zealand. Banks and businesses ceased to give the Church further credit, and some of the Marist priests and brothers expressed the opinion that they were overworked, under-resourced and unappreciated. Nor were they able to participate in anything like the religious community life which they envisaged when they joined their religious order. One of them, Father Petitjean, wrote to Jean-Claude Colin, the Marist Superior in Lyon:

'Our bishop . . . had from afar a brilliant reputation for ability, confidence, a fortune and even noble blood. But he does not appear

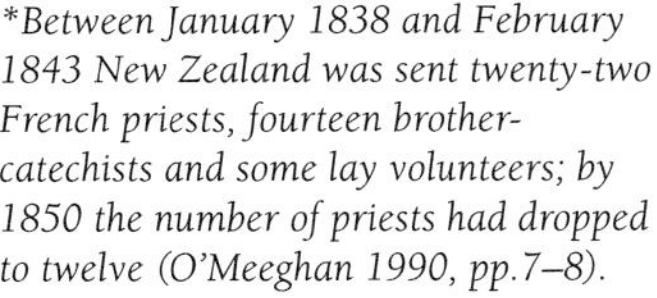

**Between January 1838 and February 1843 New Zealand was sent twenty-two French priests, fourteen brother-catechists and some lay volunteers; by 1850 the number of priests had dropped to twelve (O'Meeghan 1990, pp.7–8).*

to be reliable in his words, promising too much, quite rash in business, banking on the future and consuming loans, laying little of solid foundation, easy to charm, flatter and catch unawares, or at least yielding to everyone because he wishes to make use of everything and win all. He conceived gigantic enterprises, such as wishing to build a church in brick, to buy a boat and keep it in the repair in which it was . . . We are like an army that has used up part of its ammunition in fireworks.'[35]

❖

The most difficult feature to assess of the mission's early years is the fruit of its proselytising among Maori. Figures quoted in letters for prospective conversions tend to be recklessly optimistic. In 1841, after nearly four years of evangelising, the number of Catholic Maori in New Zealand was around only 1000 — in a total population of perhaps 100,000. At the same time the Protestant mission claimed about 2000 Maori converts; and the number of Pakeha Catholics was 765.

As Pompallier himself reported on several occasions, the most spectacular results in religious recruitment tended to accompany or follow the conversion of chiefs — who sometimes brought their families and followers into the Church. This had happened in the case of Rewa at Kororareka in 1839; with Moka at Opotiki the following year supposedly bringing in 600 potential converts; and with Korakai at Rotorua (400–500).[36]

But, as became clear in retrospect, early expressions of enthusiasm often represented no more than excitement generated by some of the famous debates between Marist and Protestant clergy — such as that which occurred near Opotiki between Father Joseph Chouvet and John Alexander Wilson, a CMS missionary. Father Chouvet, who was accompanied by Father Lampila, wrote:

'We rolled in front of the natives a big chart which has as a title "The Tree of the Church". Then we showed them on this chart the establishment of the Church by our Lord Jesus Christ, the choice that the divine master made of Saint Peter as leader or pope, and the uninterrupted government of this same church by the successors of Saint Peter down to Gregory XVI, who was then reigning.

'We called this tree the ladder of the Catholics, by means of which they could go back to Saint Peter, and consequently, to Jesus Christ . . . I read out loud the names of all the popes written on this chart. This reading charmed the natives who are very fond of genealogical recitals, and vie with each other as to who can recite the greatest number of known ancestors' names . . . Then turning towards my adversary, I spoke to him in this fashion:

"Well! friend, since you boast that like us you descend from Jesus Christ, show us your genealogical tree or ladder."

'Finally, defeated and overcome by the inexorable demand: "Give us, give us your ladder!" he let slip these despairing words: "Our ladder, we have lost it." Then the audience . . . burst out laughing, and replied to him ironically: "Ah! you have lost your ladder. Well! look for it." This incident . . . made more of an impression on the minds of the natives than all the discussions we could have made to prove the truth and the divinity of the faith.'[37]

The Maori converts who held to their religion most tenaciously tended to be those who lived in communities that had become Catholic *en masse* such as those in the northern Hokianga and — at a later period — on the Whanganui River. A large number of other individuals left the Church when wars occurred and the mission was identified as 'Pakeha' (as happened in the North in 1845–46 and in Taranaki, Waikato and the Bay of Plenty in 1863–65); or when they had opportunities to join other religions, which seemed more active or more interested in their own tribe and neighbourhood.

Sometimes genuine acts of Maori piety or worship were misunderstood by European priests, who may have viewed such matters through the prism of their own culture. When an Arawa carver named Patoromu Tamatea carved a Maori Madonna and child for the newly built chapel in the Bay of Plenty, he indicated the status and the virginity of the Virgin Mary in Maori terms by giving her a full facial moko. The priest to whom the tekoteko was then offered refused to accept it and indicated that he found it sacrilegious, even blasphemous.[38] Pompallier himself may not have responded in this manner: he spoke to his priests of the need to build Catholic belief around existing Maori tikanga or custom and to avoid seeing Maori ideas as anti-Christian simply because they were non-European.[39] But the fact is that such misunderstandings occurred; and when they did they were likely to diminish Maori commitment to Christianity.

There were also, in the 1840s and 1850s, remarkably few Maori recruits for Catholic religious vocations. One of those few, a woman named Hoki, baptised Peata (Beata), was a niece of the Kororareka chief Rewa. She had borne a child before her baptism in 1839 but remained celibate after conversion. She joined the northern mission as a lay worker in the 1840s. In 1850 she went to Wellington with the newly appointed Bishop Viard, then returned to Auckland to enter the Sisters of Mercy in 1851. She was joined there by another Maori postulant, Ateraita, a Ngati Awa woman from Whakatane. Two novices, Erahia from Whangaroa and Ropina from Rotorua, followed them in 1862,

Sister Peata (centre) of Ngapuhi, first Maori nun, with her French protégée Sister Suzanne Aubert and Maori pupils at the Nazareth Institute in Auckland. Peata was by this time close to blindness. This photograph was commissioned by Bishop Pompallier when planning a history of his mission.
~ Sisters of Compassion

but are believed to have left the order during the wars of the mid-1860s. There appear to have been no other Maori candidates for the religious life at this time.

Letters from priests in the early years of the mission, especially those isolated in Maori communities, are often redolent of strain and fatigue. 'Our little house had served, they tell me, as a sty for pigs,' Father Borjon wrote to Father Colin from Maketu in 1842. 'We can scarcely keep our lamp alight or find enough covering at night to stop us becoming too cold. Chests serve as a bed.'[40]

The rare descriptions of others who saw the missionaries in the field are even bleaker. A traveller in the Bay of Plenty, for example, came upon Father Pezant on Papamoa Beach in December 1842: 'I never remember seeing a more miserable figure — Travel worn unshaven & unwashed he wore the tricornered hat of his order, his long coat & a kind of black petticoat [was] tucked up with the Skirts under the waistband and a pair of old Wellington boots were drawn over his trousers. From his neck hung a large crucifix and on his back a kind of sack containing in all probability all he possessed in the world.'[41] The impression lingers of a man who is far from home, out of context, and — at least at this moment in his life — out of countenance.

But there were compensations. If missionary journeys were difficult and uncomfortable, Michel Borjon wrote (and they were), they were also truly Apostolic. '[And] what happy graces for souls and for ourselves! Here are fought face to face, heresy, infidelity, and here are these people taught the truths of Salvation . . . These people are sometimes so eager for religious instruction that in the light of big fires, one stays up till 10 and 11 o'clock . . . After these trips the Missionary returns happily to his place of residence . . . There he repairs his physical and spiritual forces, studies the language, theology, writes prayer books . . . [He] gives instruction morning and evening at prayers, thus leading the life of a Pastor . . . [How] beautiful in the eyes of Faith . . .'[42]

Seven months later thirty-year-old Father Borjon was dead, drowned at sea off East Cape.

CHAPTER TWO

A French Church?

THE ESTABLISHMENT of the Nanto-Bordelaise colony on Banks Peninsula had not led, as some French authorities had hoped, to the French annexation of the South Island of New Zealand. The settlers had arrived in August 1840 to find that the British Government had usurped such an opportunity by proclaiming its own sovereignty over the whole country three months before.

The French immigrants and a minority of Germans, fifty-three in all, nevertheless established what was at first a viable French community at Akaroa. Bishop Pompallier visited in October 1840. He had assigned Fathers Jean-Baptiste Comte and André Tripe (a French diocesan priest) and Brother Florentin to minister to the colonists. Within a short time they had built a church and started a school. Thus Akaroa became the first European station in the New Zealand Catholic mission, and Pompallier and his culture-starved priests initially enjoyed their association with it (the opportunities to speak French, read French books, eat French cuisine, drink wine).

Opposite ~ French Marists in characteristic dress and posture on the Maori mission trail ~ Fathers Christophe Soulas and Pierre Broussard inspect the remnants of Father Jean-Baptiste Comte's mission at Pukekaraka, Otaki.
~ Marist Archives

Saint Patrick's Church, Akaroa, built in 1865. This was the third Catholic church raised in the Banks Peninsula French community. Unlike its predecessors it survives after more than 130 years.
~ Marist Archives

In 1841 the bishop stayed in Akaroa while the *Sancta Maria* was undergoing a refit for its forthcoming voyage to the islands, a process which some of his priests felt was unnecessary. While he was waiting, Pompallier wrote a Maori catechism and summary of doctrine, *Ako Marama o Te Hahi Katorika Romana*, which would be used extensively by the Catholic Maori missioners. Fathers Comte and Tripe also claimed to have converted 'a significant enough proportion' of the 300 Maori on Banks Peninsula (ninety-eight in all), including the infant son of the chief Iwikau, and other chiefs, such as Tiemi Nohomutu and Apera Pukenui.[1]

The Akaroa station did not long survive, however. The priests left in 1842 — Father Comte and Brother Florentin in March and Father Tripe in November — because of strong Protestant competition for the Maori congregation and religious apathy among the French colonists. Tripe was so traumatised by the experience that he returned to France. Priests continued to visit the peninsula intermittently, especially the robust Comte, who was based among Maori at Otaki from 1844 to 1854. Akaroa did not become a parish with its own priest until 1880. Significantly that priest was an Irishman, Father J. A. Donovan.

The mission's second European station was opened in Auckland in October 1842 by Father Jean-Baptiste Petitjean. By January 1843, in what became the common pattern for development, a wooden church was open and doubling as a school (the roll was 155 by 1845 and twice this two years later). Father Jean Forest joined Petitjean there in 1842, and they were assisted by Father Séon, who was responsible for Auckland Maori and later for the fledgling community of Onehunga. The establishment in 1848 and 1849 of four Fencible settlements — to protect Auckland from possible Maori attack — swelled the European population on the isthmus to over 1000. These troops had been recruited largely in Ireland and hence their presence also increased the number of Auckland Catholics. Consequently Father Garin was put in charge of new villages at Howick, Panmure and Otahuhu. Bishop Pompallier moved his own headquarters to Auckland when he returned in 1850 from a four-year visit to Europe. He was greeted by the sight of the first Saint Patrick's Cathedral, a hammered scoria church and the largest and most permanent building so far erected for the New Zealand Catholic mission, which had been consecrated in 1848.

Over the same period a third European station was being developed at Port Nicholson, the New Zealand Company settlement at the base of the North Island, which was later known as Wellington. It had a high proportion of English and Irish

Saint Patrick's Cathedral, Auckland, built in scoria and opened in 1848. At the time it was the largest permanent building in the New Zealand Catholic mission. It was absorbed into a new church on the same site, dedicated in 1907. ~ *Auckland Diocese*

Catholics from 1840. Indeed, so great was the involvement of aristocratic English families in its establishment that Wellington almost became a specifically Catholic colony. Bishop Pompallier made his first pastoral visit there in December 1840 and celebrated Mass at the home of the magistrate, Michael Murphy. Other prominent members of the congregation included an Irish surgeon named John Patrick Fitzgerald, who assumed leadership of the Catholic community until a priest arrived, and Baron G. E. von Alzdorf, a German businessman. There was also an English aristocrat, Henry Petre, who would soon be joined by two of his cousins, William Vavasour and Charles Clifford — all three of them members of ancient English Catholic families who were to give considerable social and financial support to the Church in Wellington in its early years.

AKO MARAMA

O TE HAHI KATORIKA ROMANA

KO TE

POU ME TE UNGA

O TE PONO.

Maku e ho atu ki a koe nga ki o te rangatiratanga o te rangi.

MATIU 16. 19.

KORORAREKA :

HE MEA TA I TE PEREHI O TE WIKARIATU APOTORIKO O TE OHEANIA OKIHETARI, I TE MARAMA OKOTOPA.

1842.

So fast did Wellington grow (2500 settlers by 1841, 4000 by 1843) that Pompallier undertook to appoint a priest there. The sixth contingent of French Marists for the New Zealand mission arrived in Wellington in April 1842 and stayed there five days before heading north. Four months later, while the bishop was still in the Islands, Father Borjon and Brother Déodat were despatched from Auckland to open a Wellington station. They were never seen again. Several weeks later wreckage washed up on the east coast was identified as coming from their ship, the *Speculator*.[2]

By extraordinary coincidence the same day that the *Speculator* left Auckland another vessel, the *Thomas Sparkes*, set sail for Wellington from England with another priest on board. He was Jeremiah Purcell O'Reily, an Irish Capuchin (a branch of the Franciscan order). Father O'Reily, thirty-seven years old, had been well educated in France and Italy, was an accomplished classical scholar, and had a record of fine preaching and solid pastoral work in Cork, Dublin and Kilkenny. He had been recruited as Catholic chaplain to the New Zealand Company settlement by Lord Petre, a director of the company and father of Henry Petre.

Father O'Reily arrived in Wellington on 31 January 1843 with Henry Petre (who had returned to England to marry); and with Petre's bride, Mary Walmsley, and horses (Aether and Riddlesworth), peacocks and pheasants. The priest said his first Mass there on 5 February in front of a congregation of 100 gathered in Baron von Alzdorf's waterfront hotel. 'He had made particular preparation for the occasion,' O'Reily's biographer noted, by 'having his white hair cut off and wearing a red wig, which was to be called into service on special occasions in the future.'[3]

In addition to English Catholics, Father O'Reily wrote two months later, he was delighted to find 'some of my poor countrymen from Erin's most distant shores, and it cheered me

Father Jeremiah O'Reily, the Irish Capuchin engaged by Lord Petre as chaplain to the New Zealand Company settlement at Port Nicholson. Later in his life, by the time this portrait was taken, he was highly venerated and known as the Apostle of Wellington.
~ *Marist Archives*

to let them see, if I could do nothing else, the solicitude of the Church in their regard. They are, in truth, like the Jews, scattered everywhere; but not . . . broken and disconnected . . . The poor people have no chapel here as yet, nor have they means of providing one. Up to the present we have been saying Mass in a room adjoining a public house; we are lately removed to an old store on the beach.'[4]

Pompallier had known nothing of O'Reily's appointment, nor of his arrival in the colony. But he willingly granted the Irishman his faculties (episcopal permission to exercise his ministry) when the priest wrote and announced his presence. And, indeed, the bishop must eventually have been highly pleased with the calibre of the unexpected recruit. In numerical terms O'Reily replaced the lost Borjon. But his level of education was probably superior to that of most of the Marists and he had had extensive pastoral experience.

Father O'Reily turned out to be an unusually effective preacher, a diplomat in his dealings with his Protestant neighbours and an effective fund raiser. He had a chapel ready by mid-1843 and the first Saint Mary of the Angels by 1874. The first Catholic school opened in 1847 in the original chapel with the sanctuary area curtained off. O'Reily also took initial responsibility, with Father Comte in Otaki, for much of the surrounding districts, including the upper half of the South Island (until Father Garin was appointed to Nelson in 1850). Francis Redwood, who was five years old when he first saw O'Reily celebrate Mass in his parents' house at Waimea in 1844, stated that his family venerated the Irish priest 'almost as an angel from Heaven'.[5] Thirty years later Redwood would himself come to Wellington, as O'Reily's bishop and ecclesiastical superior.

Notre-Dame de La Salette
Vierge en pleurs

O'Reily remained on close terms too with those of his parishioners who became powerful figures in the political life of the colony. Charles Clifford, for example, went on to become a member of the Legislative Council in 1844 and the Wellington Provincial Council in 1853, and the first Speaker of the House of Representatives in 1854 (responsible for introducing the prayer which is still said at the beginning of each sitting of the New Zealand Parliament). Henry Petre became Colonial Treasurer and Postmaster General in 1853. A Catholic cousin of Clifford's, Frederick Weld, who arrived in Wellington in 1844, went on to become Premier of New Zealand in 1864. John Patrick Fitzgerald became Colonial Surgeon and his brother Thomas became first Superintendent of the province of Hawke's Bay. Sectarian feeling meant that such achievements by Catholics in public life would have been unlikely at this time in the United Kingdom. They were a measure of the considerably greater degree of religious tolerance established in the new colony — a tolerance for which Bishop Pompallier, and Father O'Reily and his Wellington co-religionists, must take much of the credit.

When Rome decided in 1848 to split the New Zealand Church into two administrative units, everywhere south of Taupo eventually becoming part of the new Port Nicholson Diocese, Father O'Reily was well qualified to become the country's second Catholic bishop. The promotion never came, however. The Holy See, acting on advice from Pompallier, gave the new diocese to Philippe Viard — who, while he lacked the Irishman's learning and flair, had been appointed Pompallier's auxiliary in 1846 and shown himself to be a reliable and loyal deputy. Instead, Viard appointed Father O'Reily his Vicar General and paid him the highest tribute one man could make to another: '[He] has befriended without effort the entire population. And how could he not be the friend of all, he who never grieved anyone? He is for clergy and people an example of the sweetness, humility, charity and resignation of our Divine Saviour . . .'[6] In a reorganised diocese, Father O'Reily remained parish priest of Te Aro in Wellington until 1878. He died full of years and honour in 1880.

His early colleague Father Jean-Baptiste Comte, sent to Wellington in 1844 to be responsible for the Maori mission in the region, did not stay the course. Comte went north to Otaki to proselytise among the Ngati Kapumanawhiti, Ngati Huia and Muaupoko, and among tribes to the north and south of his base (the neighbouring Ngati Raukawa and Ngati Toa had largely gone over to the Anglican Church after Octavius Hadfield established his CMS station at Otaki in 1839). Working from a hill named Pukekaraka, which had in pre-European times been a tuahu or holy place used by tohunga, Father Comte initially had spectacular success. Local chiefs were baptised (Te Ra, Tonihi) and another highly respected man, Hakaraia Rangikura, became a catechist.

Father François Melu, who re-opened Jean-Baptiste Comte's mission at Pukekaraka and lived there himself for more than forty years.
~ *Marist Archives*

When Bishop Viard first visited the station in 1850 he found 200 Catholic Maori there.

Buoyed by this apparent spiritual progress, Comte made strenuous efforts to make his flock materially secure. He established vast areas of market garden and bought a schooner to carry produce to Wellington for sale. He built a water mill soon after raising a small church, and a school in which he taught. But the very success of his enterprises carried the seeds of what he viewed as his downfall. '[He] became so concerned with not being able to reconcile his religious priesthood with the money-making involved in his development project' that he resigned his post and returned to France, where he worked as a diocesan priest for the next forty years.[7] Nobody was immediately available to replace him. Fathers Séon and Moreau and others tried to keep the mission alive through periodic visits from other places; and in 1859 they completed the new church that, according to local tradition, Comte had started building in 1852 (which survives as the oldest Catholic church in the country). But, with Comte's departure the mission collapsed and would not be effectively revived until Father François Melu began visiting the area from Turakina in the 1880s and finally settled at Pukekaraka in 1890 (remaining there until his retirement in 1935).

Mater Admirabilis ~ A French Madonna

Meanwhile Maori missions in the North were now in decline. Hone Heke's war in 1845–46 had not been directed at Catholics. Indeed, Catholic mission buildings were spared when Kororareka was sacked in March 1845; and Ngapuhi rangatira had asked Pompallier to mediate between Hone and the Imperial forces. Nevertheless the fighting had the effect of making many Maori withdraw from the Christian Churches which, since clergy had ministered to Imperial troops, Maori were now inclined to view as Pakeha institutions. Father Baty's Maori congregation at Kororareka was replaced by one of 200 soldiers marched to Mass with a musical escort. Practice of the Faith among Maori languished in the Bay of Islands, at Whangaroa and Mangakahia. Only the northern Hokianga communities remained largely loyal to the Whakapono, and even here there was some falling away. The Auckland Maori mission run by Father Séon from 1845 to 1850 (among his other responsibilities, which included from 1847 being chaplain to the Onehunga Fencible settlement) was not markedly more successful. The conversion rate was not high. Saint Mary's on the North Shore opened as a boarding school for Maori boys but was later transferred to Ponsonby, where its enrolments were never as numerous as Séon and Pompallier had expected.

It was in the Waikato among the Tainui tribes that real progress continued. Father Jean Pezant took over there in 1844 and moved his central station from Matamata, where results had been

negligible, to Rangiaowhia. Over the next two decades, under Pezant to 1850 and Father Joseph Garavel to 1863, 1100 Maori were baptised, and large numbers confirmed and married. Garavel built a large church and a successful school, and he persuaded the tribes around Rangiaowhia to establish extensive market gardens, as Comte had done in Otaki, and to build mills for the grinding and export of flour. The prosperity thus induced among both Catholic and Anglican Maori in the Waikato made this period in the late 1850s and early 1860s one that Tainui would look back on as a 'golden age'. The Waikato war of the mid-1860s brought an end to this intensive religious and economic florescence. It was never revived on the same scale. Sadly, one of the worst atrocities of the war, involving the raping of women by British troops and the burning to death of a number of women, children and old people, took place in Rangiaowhia and was never forgotten. It was an incident that helped the growth of Pai Marire in the Waikato and made many Tainui Maori reluctant to rejoin Christian Churches in the nineteenth and early twentieth century.[8]

For its first forty years the Opotiki mission had a series of raupo chapels ~ in effect, small meeting houses. Here Father James McDonald stands with his congregation in front of one of the later ones. This station was described as 'poor and insufficient' in a diocesan report made soon after this visit.
~ *Auckland Diocese*

The Rotorua station too had prospered in the years prior to the wars of the 1860s. Father Euloge Reignier went there from Opotiki in 1843 and moved the headquarters to Ohinemutu,

Interior of Saint Joseph's, Otumoetai, headquarters of the Tauranga station opened by Philippe Viard and the catechist Romano in 1840. This chapel, built by 1850 and lined with tukutuku panels, was regarded as a fine example of its kind. The Tauranga Catholic population included six Frenchmen who had married into Maori families.
~ A. C. Bellamy

heartland of the Arawa people. From here he covered an area bordered by Maketu, Rotorua and Taupo; and by 1849 he had baptised 1300 Maori. Results from the Bay of Plenty stations — Tauranga, Whakatane, Opotiki — were less spectacular. Fathers Pezant, Bernard, Lampila (who ranged over an area from Matata to Hawke's Bay), Chouvet and Moreau did well enough to justify their presence and enjoyed some occasional coups, such as Chouvet's victory in debate with the Reverend J. A. Wilson in 1844. And the number of Catholic Maori in Waikato and the Bay of Plenty was at least increasing at a time when they were diminishing in the previously fertile Far North.

❖

When Bishop Pompallier arrived in Auckland in April 1850 after a four-year visit to Europe he was returning to a Church very different from the one he had established in New Zealand twelve years before. He had cut all formal ties with the Marist order. He was no longer responsible for the missions of Western Oceania. Now there was to be one northern New Zealand diocese based on the Auckland province, which he would administer with the assistance of secular clergy; and one diocese south of Taupo, which Philippe Viard would supervise from Wellington, initially as Apostolic Administrator, later as bishop, with the help of his Marist confrères who would join him there. The nature of this split and the shape of the new administration was largely a consequence of the breakdown of Pompallier's relations with the Marists.

The bishop brought with him from Europe one ordained minister and ten student priests. Within five weeks all but one of the students were ordained — Pompallier needed to put them into the field as soon as possible to replace the Marists; and they, along with two English clergy who had found their own way to New Zealand and the one already ordained, gave the bishop a total of eleven priests. By the middle of April 1850 most of the Marists had gone and the new team of diocesan clergy had been assigned to Onehunga, the Bay of Islands, Waikato, Tauranga and Opotiki. The Hokianga was to be serviced for a period from the Bay of Islands.

The training and ordination of the first group of students in New Zealand in 1850 also marked the beginning of the first local seminary, which moved from the North Shore to Ponsonby in 1852. Over the next seventeen years it would graduate twenty priests, all of them European and some of them already part-trained in Ireland or France. The college also educated Maori catechists, some of whom were encouraged to stay on for training for the priesthood. Fifteen Maori students took this opportunity and one — Keremeti Pine from Okaihau — was even sent to Rome where for three years, among seminarians from Africa and Asia, he studied Latin and spoke passable Italian. But no Maori candidate for the priesthood was ordained at this time.*[9] In addition Pompallier had arranged with All Hallows Seminary in Drumcondra near Dublin, a specifically missionary college, to take two of their priests each year; this was the beginning of a long and growing association between Irish seminaries — All Hallows, Cloyne, Maynooth, Kilkenny — and the Church in New Zealand.

In spite of all this effort, however, Pompallier's experience with the Marists was to be largely repeated: his lofty manner and his continuing inability to organise finances meant that, with several notable exceptions, he was to be no more successful maintaining harmonious relations with his new priests than he had been with his earlier ones.

With nuns, however, the bishop fared far better — not so much because of their attitude to him, perhaps, as his to them. With religious women, as with Maori, he seemed to be at his best: the charming, confident and wise teacher who felt no need to be

Prayer of
Saint Ignatius Loyola

Dearest Lord, teach me to be generous: to serve Thee as Thou deservest to be served, to give without counting the cost, to fight without heeding the wounds, to toil without seeking rest, to labour without seeking any other than the knowledge that I do Thy holy will, O Lord.

*Unlike the Protestant Churches, which were ordaining Maori from the mid-nineteenth century, the Catholic Church did not ordain a Maori priest until Father Wiremu Te Awhitu, in 1944 — 106 years after the beginning of Catholic evangelising.

autocratic. He had brought with him from Ireland in 1850 Mother Cecilia Maher and seven sisters from the Sisters of Mercy convent in Carlow. They respected, admired, even loved their bishop; and he seems at all times to have acted graciously and thoughtfully towards them. Within a week of arriving in Auckland they were plunged straight into teaching Catholic children, looking after orphans and instructing women and girls in the Faith. To this initial inventory they soon added prison visits (many of the town's early criminals, especially those committing alcohol-related offences, turned out to be Irish and Catholic); nursing sick mothers and children in their homes; and taking in laundry and sewing for income in addition to that received from the provincial government for teaching and from the bishop.

First Communion Certificate, Saint Patrick's Cathedral, Auckland, 1858

The sisters also began at once to learn Maori and soon had a number of Maori girls in the boarding establishment of their first school. Sister Philomena wrote: 'I am quite enraptured by the New Zealanders. There are six Native girls in the house at present, one of them has a beautiful tattooed face. They are simple, innocent, pious, not rude but on the contrary very gentle and respectful to superiors . . . [Some] are so tall that it would be almost necessary for me to mount a ladder to see their purty tattooed faces . . . now I am . . . accustomed to tattooed faces, blankets for cloaks, no shoes or coats, no stockings, no hats & sometimes a mat for a cloak . . .'[10]

In 1853 Bishop Pompallier bought a 40-acre property in Ponsonby and named it Mount Saint Mary's. This was to be (and a vestige of it remains) the administrative centre of the Auckland Diocese. An existing house became the first bishop's residence on the site and was replaced forty years later with a more imposing brick-built Bishop's House (called for a time, in the usage of the day, a 'palace'). The Sisters of Mercy made their headquarters on the site and subsequently built a large convent and boarding school there, Saint Mary's, after the bishop had made over half the property to them. From there the order grew in numbers and influence, recruiting New Zealand postulants and welcoming reinforcements from Ireland. They opened further convents in Parnell and Onehunga; and, in 1861, they established the order in Wellington.

For Pompallier, however, the most welcome Irish recruits to the diocese were the brothers McDonald: James, who arrived from All Hallows in 1852; and Walter, who came in 1856 and was ordained that year by his New Zealand bishop. Both men had been born at Mooncoin; both longed to serve as missionaries; and both formed close and trusting relationships with Pompallier. Both also attracted exceptional loyalty and affection from their respective parishioners. James was diocesan Vicar General from

Father Walter McDonald ~ private secretary to Bishop Pompallier and one of his most loyal supporters from 1856 to 1869. Subsequently he was an immensely popular parish priest at Panmure from 1886 to 1899. ~ *Auckland Diocese*

1853 until the bishop's retirement in 1869, when he became first parish priest of Drury and then, from 1880 to 1890, Vicar General to Maori in the Auckland Diocese. Walter became the bishop's private secretary until 1869, then administrator of the diocese until 1886, and finally parish priest at Panmure until his death in 1899. They were followed closely to New Zealand from Ireland by Fathers James Paul, who served mainly in Onehunga, Michael O'Hara, who would be parish priest at Onehunga for thirty-six years, and Patrick O'Brien who was not a success and would eventually be dismissed for persistent drunkenness.

Pompallier and the McDonalds ran the Auckland Diocese as a troika for more than a decade. The positive feature of this arrangement was that it was harmonious (among themselves at least) and that progress was made establishing new parishes on the outskirts of Auckland central. 'Bishop's House, the Church of the Immaculate Conception, the Convent of the Holy Family and the school and orphanage of the Sisters of Mercy grew up as a sort of Catholic colony on Mount Saint Mary in Ponsonby. Suburban churches and schools were built and grew strong.'[11]

The negative effect was that neither of the Fathers McDonald was any better at managing money than Pompallier. Many of the diocesan school and church properties became progressively debt-ridden: as money was received it was eaten up in interest payments and repayment of principal. The McDonalds seemed unable to persuade the bishop to change methods of management he had used for his entire episcopal career — indeed, as criticism grew from both priests and laity, the loyal brothers simply defended Pompallier's decisions and contributed to his feeling that he was being besieged by unworthy, visionless adversaries.

Confirmation Certificate, Saint Patrick's Cathedral, Auckland, 1858

When the bishop returned to Europe in 1859, some of his most prominent Auckland laymen would have been only too happy had he stayed away and stepped aside for a successor. 'Peter Grace said that if the Bishop was coming back they would soon make a petition to the Pope to keep him,' Father Garavel, temporarily recalled to Auckland, wrote in his journal. '[Patrick] Dignan said that the reason why they did not present an address was because they must put some thing wrong [that is, uncomplimentary] in it.'[12] Grace and Dignan had made considerable contributions to the financing of Saint Patrick's church and Auckland's Catholic schools.

Far from contemplating resignation the bishop returned to Auckland in December 1860 with eight Italian Franciscans (six priests and two brothers), eight seminarians, including his nephew Antoine Pompallier, and four French laywomen, including his niece Lucie Pompallier and the redoubtable 'Napoleon in petticoats', Suzanne Aubert — who, like the Pompalliers, was Lyonnais. The Franciscans were to take over the North Shore College and be responsible for Maori missions north of Auckland. The Frenchwomen, after attaching themselves briefly and unsuccessfully to the Sisters of Mercy, formed their own order, the Congregation of the Holy Family, in 1862. They took over the care and education of Maori children in a boarding school known as the Nazareth Institute. Here too they professed New Zealand's first Maori nuns, Sisters Peata and Ateraita, whom they had taken with them from the Mercy sisters.

Both the Italians and the French sisters created new problems for the bishop, however. The Franciscans, though they were wholly unprepared for the Maori mission, resented having to go north with Father Garavel, who was to introduce them to their Maori flock. Then, halfway through 1861, the Franciscan superior, Ottavio Barsanti, moved his North Shore community into a house in central Auckland, because he and his confrères objected to being so far away from 'civilisation'. They did not seek permission

Bishop Pompallier in his later years ~ still a charismatic preacher and teacher, but progressively crippled by a combination of obesity and rheumatism.
~ *Holy Cross College*

from the bishop to relocate. When Vicar General James McDonald told Father Barsanti that this was an excommunicable offence, the turbulent Italian knocked him sprawling and sent a chalice flying through the cathedral sacristy.

Pompallier stripped Barsanti of his authority; but, in an effort to make peace, he gave the Franciscans the new parish of Parnell. Father Barsanti left New Zealand for Australia in 1866; from there, after being suspended for drunkenness and physical violence, he tried to have himself appointed Bishop of Auckland. In a cruel irony, Rome asked his opinion on James McDonald's suitability for promotion to bishop and received a devastating reply. Other Franciscans, especially Dominic Galosi and Stephen Passinetti, continued to staff the Purakau and Russell mission stations until the order withdrew from New Zealand in 1873. From that time until James McDonald's appointment as Vicar General to the Maori in 1880, Maori Catholics in the Far North were all but abandoned by the Catholic Church.[13]

The Nazareth Institute languished as the number of Maori children fell away sharply after the outbreak of the Waikato war. Maori catechists and seminarians also withdrew from the seminary as Tainui and other tribes recalled their people from Auckland, and especially from their large settlement at Mangere, as the Government demanded that they take sides for or against the Maori King, Tawhiao. Tawhiao himself had been on the verge of conversion to Catholicism in 1862 but pulled back when the Government initiated hostilities against his people in 1863.[14]

In addition, Pompallier mortgaged the property on which the Nazareth Institute stood. This meant that when Suzanne Aubert and her sisters thought they were paying off the property to secure ownership they were in fact only meeting interest payments. By the late 1860s Aubert had taken a strong dislike to her bishop, to James McDonald, and to the entire community of the Sisters of Mercy. She fought to keep the school for Maori girls open at a time when economic recession and the withdrawal of Maori from Auckland led the diocesan authorities to believe that such an institution was no longer justifiable. Lucie Pompallier, nominally superior of the sisters at the Nazareth Institute, appears not to

The Marist mission at Meeanee in Hawke's Bay, to which Suzanne Aubert retreated from Auckland in 1871, was in many respects a tiny island of French culture. The priests and brothers there spoke French to one another, read French books and established New Zealand's first commercial vineyard ~ with an initial emphasis on the production of altar wine. In the early years of the twentieth century the vineyard and community were moved to nearby Greenmeadows to escape winter floods.
~ Marist Archives

have supported her compatriot. She left New Zealand with her uncle in 1868 in the wake of suggestions that she had become emotionally involved with one of the diocesan priests, Father Paul Sarda (who, after being banished by Pompallier, drowned in the wreck of the *General Grant* en route for Europe).[15] Pompallier's successor, Bishop Thomas Croke, forbade Aubert to continue as a religious in Auckland and tried to persuade her to return to France. Instead, she went south in 1871 to join Father Euloge Reignier and his team of Marist priests and brothers at Meeanee in Hawke's Bay. There she began a new phase of her life as a healer, a maker of patent medicines and an exceptionally active and loved missionary among the Maori.

Pompallier's financial difficulties had compounded. The combination of the removal of the capital to Wellington in 1865 and the effects of the Waikato war had created an economic slump in Auckland. Church income dropped along with government and local body revenue and the wages of parishioners. In these circumstances the bishop's practice of operating on credit and spending money before he had raised it was even more risky than it had been previously. By 1868 he was in debt to the order of £7000. He was also old, sick, tired and feeling more than ever under siege. In the wake of a stormy meeting of creditors and laymen he decided to go to Europe to seek financial help. Four months after his departure his creditors forced a sale of all the furnishings in Bishop's House, 'down to the carpet rings and bedding'.[16] Pompallier was mortified when he heard. Along with rumours circulating of alleged drunkenness and sexual misconduct, it was too much.* He resigned his see feeling rejected and unappreciated and retired to Puteaux, a suburb of Paris, to be looked after by his niece Lucie. He died there on 1 December 1871.

In the Wellington Diocese to which Viard had withdrawn in 1850 with his band of Marists (some of them most unwilling to leave their established stations and work among the Maori), the rate of evangelisation seemed at first especially promising as priests fanned out into new districts.

Father Jean Lampila took two brothers with him to visit Gisborne and then open a Hawke's Bay station at Pakowhai between Napier and Hastings (it was later shifted to Meeanee). Father Reignier joined them in 1851 and ranged widely around the region, as far south as Woodville. The following year Fathers Pezant and Bernard opened a Wanganui mission and Father Lampila transferred from Hawke's Bay to establish another station

*These rumours, reported to Bishop Aloysius Goold of Melbourne (asked by Rome to investigate Pompallier's affairs), were entirely without evidential foundation. They were symptomatic of the atmosphere of recrimination which prevailed in Auckland after Pompallier's departure.

Philippe Viard, Maori missionary and subsequently first Catholic Bishop of Wellington. He was in his fifties when this portrait was taken but, like many of his early Marist colleagues, he looked considerably older.
~ *Auckland Diocese*

Pompallier's grave at Puteaux, a suburb of Paris, where the bishop died in 1871 in the care of his devoted niece. The man alongside is l'Abbé Delouvrier, parish priest of Puteaux in 1984.
~ *Auckland Diocese*

among Maori up the Whanganui River, at Kaiwhaiki, then from 1854 at Kauaeroa, across the river from Hiruharama (Jerusalem). There he built a chapel, a school and a flour mill. He made good progress converting local Maori, many of whom had previously been Anglican. (The CMS missionary Richard Taylor even accused Lampila of encouraging Hiruharama Maori to dismantle the Anglican chapel there to provide timber for the Catholic one at Kauaeroa.) According to Whanganui Maori tradition, the statue of the Blessed Virgin in the chapel at Kauaeroa was seen to weep real tears.[17]

In Wellington itself Bishop Viard had a foundation stone laid for his cathedral by September 1850 and the same day opened a second Catholic school in the town, to be staffed by his Marist Sisters — the country's first indigenous religious order (which

lasted eleven years; when they dispersed in 1861 their work in Wellington was taken over by the Sisters of Mercy led by Mother Bernard Nixon, who had nursed in the Crimea with Florence Nightingale). Father Forest was sent to the neighbouring Hutt Valley and opened his first chapel there in August 1851. The Wairarapa to the north was gradually opened up in the 1860s and initially serviced by priests from Lower Hutt and Wellington. A resident priest was not appointed there until 1876, and the first church opened at Carterton in 1878.

In May 1850 Father Antoine Garin went to Nelson, where an active Catholic community had already opened a chapel in 1847 and a school in 1848. Father Garin, with Father Delphin Moreau as his curate, built new churches in Nelson and Waimea. They also opened a boarding school for boys in the Nelson presbytery, which offered French, Latin and algebra in addition to tuition in basic literacy and numeracy. One of the first pupils was Francis Redwood, son of Henry Redwood of Waimea West, an English convert and farmer who had been one of the leading figures in the district since his arrival in 1842.

One of eight children, Francis Redwood had been born in Staffordshire in 1839 and was three years old when the family reached New Zealand. Father Garin detected his exceptional

Saint Mary's School for boys in Nelson, which opened in the early 1850s as an extension of Father Antoine Garin's presbytery. Father Garin is the priest at right; Father William Mahoney at left; the lay teacher, centre, is a Mr Richards.
~ *Marist Archives*

Joseph Hoult, one of a number of English Catholics who settled around Nelson. Birmingham born, he reached New Zealand with his wife and six children in 1842 and farmed at Wai-iti. When a Catholic church was built at Waimea West in 1855 he supplied the timber. Hoult and his descendants supported that church and the one at Wakefield which replaced it for the next hundred years.
~ Patricia Saville

scholastic talent, nurtured it, then arranged for Francis to travel to France in 1850 for higher education. This was the beginning of the most illustrious career in the New Zealand Church. Redwood trained as a Marist near Toulon, was appointed professor of Latin and Greek at Saint Mary's College at Dundalk in Ireland, and ordained at Maynooth in 1865. After pastoral work and further teaching in Ireland and France he was appointed Bishop of Wellington in succession to Viard in 1874.

Until the 1860s, Garin's parish covered Nelson, Waimea, Buller, Marlborough and the northern West Coast of the South Island. He looked after the needs of his parishioners with spectacular energy and profound concern, and was another priest who generated exceptional respect and affection. In November 1890, eighteen months after his death, his coffin was disinterred for removal to a new chapel. The men performing what could have been a gruesome task received a shock: 'There lay the venerable priest absolutely unchanged . . . There was neither sign nor smell of corruption.'[18] Traditionally in the Catholic Church corporeal incorruptibility is seen as a sign of sainthood. Father Garin's is the only body known to have exhibited such a feature in New Zealand.

South of Nelson there were at first few Catholics — other than at Akaroa — and hence fewer priests. None had been to Otago since Pompallier's brief visit there in November 1840. After the settlement of Dunedin by Free Church of Scotland colonists in 1848, the religious character of the region was predominantly Presbyterian (the 1850 census recorded thirteen Catholics out of a population of 1182). And yet individual Catholics, such as

The body of Father Antoine Garin in Saint Mary's Church, Nelson, in April 1889. Eighteen months later when his remains were transferred to a new chapel the body was found to be incorrupt.
~ Nelson Provincial Museum

William Poppelwell, had asked for priestly visits. Consequently, in November 1850, Father Séon, who had reopened the Akaroa station, spent a fortnight in Otago saying Mass at the Poppelwells' home in the North East Valley on the outskirts of Dunedin, and at Otago Heads, Taieri, Moeraki and Waikouaiti. There were apparently few signs of Maori who had been baptised by Pompallier a decade earlier. Séon visited the region again in 1855 and 1856, this time from Wellington, and Father Petitjean came in 1857.

On that latter tour Petitjean also celebrated the first Mass in Christchurch, where he managed to gather a group of about twenty Catholics. The Akaroa mission had been forced to close again in 1851, because of a land dispute between the Church and the Canterbury Association, which had organised the colonisation of the province. Christchurch, however, gained its first resident priests — Fathers Jean Chataigner and Séon — in 1860. And their congregation was swollen immediately by the arrival of a batch of Irish immigrants. On paper their parish extended as far as Foveaux Strait, and they did manage to make further visits to the southernmost province. The two priests did not work well together, however, and Bishop Viard replaced Father Séon in 1861 with a recently arrived Marist, Claude Chervier. The new team worked harmoniously until Chataigner moved to Timaru in 1869. They serviced the communities of North and South Canterbury, opening a proper-sized church in Christchurch in 1864, and others at Lyttelton in 1865 and Akaroa in 1866.

A letter from Father Chataigner to his brother in 1860 reveals that journeys by land on foot and on horseback were still as difficult and unpleasant as they had been at the time of the foundation of the New Zealand mission. Chataigner's object was to visit a sick parishioner at Moeraki, 250 miles south of Christchurch.

Having got as far as Port Chalmers by ship, he covered the last 60 miles on foot, 'through bush, bays, valleys and over mountains and rivers . . . my little sack on my shoulder'. On the last night of this four-day expedition he found himself 'in the thickness of the forest [and] the longer I walked the more I sank into the frightful mud which had now become knee-deep'. On the summit he encountered a snow storm and survived, he believed, only because he was able to offer up his sufferings to the souls in Purgatory. 'I recited for them the office, also many rosaries . . . I think they would not have been displeased to see me shivering whilst . . . a breeze [blew] more icy than perfume . . .' When he arrived at his destination it was to find that the patient, Mrs Gleeson, had been dead for ten days. All Father Chataigner could do was comfort the widower and lead the funeral prayers.[19]

As Ernest Simmons has noted, because of the continuing need for such journeys along the frontier of European settlement in New Zealand, 'the swamps and chills of missionary life brought many of the priests to an early grave and crippled others with rheumatism at a comparatively early age. Colonial New Zealand was not a particularly healthy place . . .'[20] Some of these early missioners, such as Fathers Lampila and Forest, were described as elderly men whilst still in their forties and fifties.

The degree of activity in the Wellington Diocese in its first decade is suggestive of considerable progress — and, indeed, parishes such as those in Nelson and in Wellington itself were models of their kind (so much so that, in the case of Nelson, Viard suggested in 1858 that it become the see of a new diocese). But the extent of the bishop's responsibilities, from Taupo to Foveaux Strait, was vast. And until further Marists arrived from France in 1859 he had only nine priests to call on; and after reinforcements, only twelve. Like Pompallier, Viard was chronically short of money; unlike his senior colleague, he was cautious about spending what little he had. While he won considerable respect for his piety and tolerance, he was an indecisive administrator and lacked Pompallier's ability to compensate for his problems by firing up his subordinates and laity with inspiration and enthusiasm.

What changed these circumstances beyond recognition and brought unexpected resources into diocesan coffers was the discovery of gold in Otago in 1861 and on the West Coast of the South Island in 1864; and the intensive immigration programme promoted by New Zealand governments in the 1870s. The demographic and cultural consequences of these upheavals would transform the Catholic Church in New Zealand.

❖

Within six months of Gabriel Read discovering seven ounces of gold in the Tuapeka River there were more than 14,000 miners working Otago claims. The province's population shot up in one year from 12,000 to 30,000. A sizeable proportion of these diggers, perhaps as many as 13 percent, were Irish who made their way to Otago from either or both of the Californian and Australian goldfields. With them they brought their Irish consciousness, their sense of grievance against the English, and their religion. They also brought a small number of Irish priests, some of whom were raising money for Irish causes back in Ireland, while others may simply have been running away from scandals in their own dioceses. For Viard, making use of these 'sacerdotal itinerants' became a necessity: but it was also a risk.

Among the many businesses owned by Catholic Irish that sprang up around the West Coast goldfields in the 1860s was Sweeney's Hotel. Such permanent buildings marked the transition from goldfield to community and brought a consequent need for schools and churches.
Canterbury University

Father Delphin Moreau had been making a four-week visit to Otago when the first gold strike was announced. He successfully petitioned Viard to be allowed to remain there. By 1864 he had been joined by five other priests, two Marists and three itinerant Irish clergy. In a pastoral visit to the province in the same year the bishop blessed churches in Dunedin, Invercargill, Queenstown, Clyde, Alexandra, Lawrence and Waitahuna. Miners' gifts paid all of Viard's costs for the journey and left sufficient over for a sizeable donation towards the completion of Saint Mary's cathedral in Hill Street, Wellington (on a site occupied after 1901 by the Basilica of the Sacred Heart).

The whole process was repeated on the West Coast, where the Pakeha population grew in two years from a few dozen to 30,000. Because it was alluvial gold being mined, tent towns sprang up near rivers, old riverbeds or lake shores, and sometimes on coastal beaches. Wooden buildings — stores, bakeries, hotels, brothels, eventually cottages — would follow. Men would send for wives, partners and children, and what resulted was a proper community. Then there would be a need for schools and permanent churches.

Enthusiasm for this bonanza on the frontier infected some

priests as well as gold diggers — although priests were attracted by the challenge of the spiritual harvest, not the metallic one. Viard found that he had volunteers asking to serve on the Coast. Some were his own diocesan priests, others were Aucklanders or Australian-based clergy. In 1865 churches opened in Greymouth and Hokitika, in 1867 in Charleston and, in 1868, in Westport. That same year there were six priests on the Coast, five of them Irish in origin. Father Thomas Walsh, who had arrived in Auckland from All Hallows in 1866, established a school at Cobden then moved on to Westport in 1867, where he remained for the next sixty years. When he died in 1926 he was the last of the priests ordained by Pompallier.[21]

Irish immigrants brought Ireland with them. By the late 1860s Irish political questions — especially the issue of Irish independence from Britain — had invaded New Zealand public life. And it should be remembered that Irish loyalists, including members of the Orangemen's lodges, were as determined and as articulate about their viewpoints as the Fenian sympathisers were about theirs. Even those who were bystanders to the argument — English and Scottish settlers, for example — believed that there was something disloyal and even seditious about Irish Home Rule. The issues were debated at public meetings, in newspapers and in the country's Parliament. By 1868 Bishop Viard had felt the need to expel three of his Irish priests — Fathers Larkin, McDonough

Saint Patrick's School opened in Charleston near Westport to cater for the children of Catholic families attracted to the area by the discovery of gold in 1866. The first headmaster, at right, was Richard Delaney.
~ *Alexander Turnbull Library*

and McGirr — for taking an intemperate part in meetings and demonstrations. The bishop's view was that the Irish questions were political ones, and that priests did not become involved in politics.

The view of many of the West Coast Irish parishioners was rather different. They, like their compatriots in Otago, felt that they needed priests and bishops of their own nationality as well as of their own Faith. '[They] were sometimes exasperated by priests who had French as their first language, Maori as their second, and English as a poor third. French priests . . . continued to outnumber English-speaking priests in New Zealand until the mid-1880s.'[22] Dunedin Catholics communicated this view emphatically to Viard, and to Archbishop Polding in Sydney.

At the same time as goldfields money was beginning to mitigate Bishop Viard's financial worries there were setbacks in other parts of the diocese. The Taranaki and Hauhau wars of the 1860s interrupted evangelising among Maori in the Taranaki and Whanganui

This mock funeral procession in Hokitika in March 1868 commemorated the execution of Fenian activists in Manchester. It also resulted in the arrest of local spokesmen for the Fenian cause and the expulsion from New Zealand of Fathers John McGirr and William Larkin, goldfields priests.
~ Alexander Turnbull Library

districts. Enlarged churches opened in New Plymouth in 1862 and Wanganui in 1864, but they were largely financed by and built for Irish soldiers among the British forces.

Fighting on the Whanganui, involving the upper river tribes who had taken up the Maori Pai Marire faith and the lower river 'kupapa' or loyalist Maori, caused major rifts in Catholic Maori ranks. Rightly or wrongly, the Church was identified with the kupapa position and at least one Marist priest acted as a chaplain for the British forces. On the island of Moutoa in May 1864 a decisive battle was fought between Hauhau and Christian Maori. Father Lampila was in attendance from his nearby mission station at Kauaeroa. He was assisted by Brother Euloge Chabany. Their intention was to minister to the dying and dead. Both missionaries became caught up in the fighting, however. Father Lampila simply lay face down and prayed. Brother Euloge, who was not known in the district and was not in religious or clerical dress, was scalped and subsequently died. According to a Maori eye witness, a Pipiriki man named Te Meirei 'cut off the top of his head. Brother Euloge picked up and replaced the scalp and knelt for a few seconds, when he fell.'[23] A more dramatic Maori version of the story alleged that Euloge's whole head was severed, and that it was this which he had reached down and replaced on his own neck: understandably, this was taken as clear evidence of divine intervention.

Subsequently there was much discussion on the Whanganui as to whether or not Brother Euloge was a 'martyr for the Faith'. If he had been killed because of his Catholicism, he was deserving of canonisation as the country's first martyr. The eventual official consensus was that he was not, however. Te Meirei appears to have slain him simply because he was an anonymous Pakeha among kupapa Maori. Brother Euloge's name was among those subsequently placed on a memorial in the town of Wanganui as having 'died in defence of law and order against fanaticism and barbarism' — a description that did not endear his memory to the tribes of the upper Whanganui. But the Church would make a highly fruitful return to this area in the 1880s.

In June 1868 Bishop Viard sailed for Rome where he was to attend the First Vatican Council (which defined papal infallibility), discuss his difficulties with the Marist order and try to persuade the Vatican to create a new southern diocese in New Zealand. In the last objective he was wholly successful. The first Bishop of Dunedin, an Irish Maynooth graduate named Patrick Moran, who had been Vicar Apostolic of the Eastern Districts of the Cape of Good Hope, was duly appointed and established in Dunedin before

Viard returned to Wellington. At the same time the Wellington bishop was able to participate in the discussions about the Auckland diocese precipitated by Pompallier's resignation. In this case too a new appointment was made before Viard's return; and, again, it was an Irishman, Thomas Croke, who was given the mitre. There is no evidence that Viard was anything other than favourable to these appointments: he was not, as some of his Dunedin and West Coast parishioners believed, anti-Irish. The only project in which he was not successful was in attempting to get the young Francis Redwood appointed as his coadjutor.

Having helped to lay what he hoped would be strong foundations for the future development of the Church in New Zealand Viard arrived back in Wellington in March 1871, tired and in poor health. Like so many of his fellow priests he was prematurely aged at sixty-one. He died just over a year later, in June 1872. With his passing — widely lamented in Wellington — the missionary era in the Catholic Church's association with New Zealand had largely come to an end.

Opposite ~ Bishop Viard lies in state in his cathedral, Saint Mary's in Wellington, in June 1872. The nuns praying on each side of him are Sisters of Mercy from the neighbouring Hill Street convent. ~ *Auckland Diocese*

CHAPTER THREE

An Irish Church

TO OUTSIDERS, the nature of the Catholic Church in New Zealand appeared to alter drastically between the late 1860s and the early 1870s. Up to 1869 the Church had two French bishops and predominantly French clergy and pursued a policy of co-operation with civil authorities. By 1872 Pompallier and Viard had gone, the Church had two Irish bishops, and one of those new bishops appeared intent on stirring up sectarian feeling between Irish Catholics and their Protestant compatriots. Partly as a consequence of these leadership changes too, the number of French clergy coming to New Zealand would eventually diminish (though there was a second French influx in the 1860s, largely for the Maori mission); while the number of Irish priests and members of religious orders increased. These changes in ecclesiastical personnel, combined with the explosion in the Irish population in New Zealand as a consequence of the gold rushes and government-sponsored immigration programmes in the 1870s, would amount over time to a change in the character of the New Zealand Church.

Opposite ~ A typical parish priest at work ~ Father Matthew Fogarty in his study at Rangiora, South Canterbury. Born in Barrisokane, Ireland, ordained at Ennis in 1916, he gave his priestly life to New Zealand, living and working for four decades in the diocese of Christchurch. A family friend, Patrick O'Farrell, described him as 'big, bluff, patronising'.
~ Patrick O'Farrell

Patrick Moran, first Catholic Bishop of Dunedin, controversialist and vigorous promoter of Irish interests.
~ *Saint Dominic's Priory*

The choice of Bishops Moran and Croke to head the Dunedin and Auckland dioceses was by no means simply a reflection of demographic changes in New Zealand, however. When making episcopal appointments to British colonies, the Vatican had come to rely increasingly on the advice of the influential Cardinal Paul Cullen, Archbishop of Dublin and former Rector of the Irish College in Rome. The two new New Zealand bishops were, like the later Cardinal Patrick Moran of Sydney, protégés of Cullen: Moran had been consecrated by him at the age of thirty-two at the time of his appointment to the Cape of Good Hope; Croke had been a student at the Irish College when Cullen was Rector.

The effects of Thomas Croke's episcopate in New Zealand can be dealt with summarily. His major contribution to the Auckland diocese — and one that was of crucial importance at the time — was to restore it to a sound financial and administrative footing. He could say in 1873, with justice, that 'confidence in ecclesiastical administration has been restored'.[1] But Croke's real interests lay elsewhere. The only Auckland parishes that were flourishing at the time of his departure from New Zealand in 1874 were those near the Coromandel goldfields and on the Auckland isthmus itself. And income from Thames and Coromandel gold had gone a long way towards allowing Croke to wipe out Pompallier's debts. He had no real sympathy for the Maori pastorate, however, and little interest in rural parishes. In 1874 he resigned and the following year was appointed Archbishop of Cashel in Ireland, in which post he became 'the Lion of Cashel', a champion of Irish nationalism. His successor, the Dutch Jesuit Walter Steins, was not appointed until 1879, so that the diocese was without a bishop for over five years. Steins's episcopate too was short, just sixteen months, owing to his age (seventy-nine) and ill-health. He died in Sydney, where he was staying *en route* for Europe.

Meanwhile it was Patrick Moran of Dunedin who persisted and who, in a lengthy episcopate (twenty-six years) helped change the public face of Catholicism in New Zealand and altered the relations there between the Catholic Church and the State.

Moran arrived in Dunedin in February 1871 accompanied by an Irish priest, Father William Coleman, and ten Dominican nuns from the Sion Hill Convent in Dublin. The nuns started to teach Catholic children within days of unpacking. But living conditions, for them and their bishop, were at first decidedly substandard. Father Delphin Moreau, the Marist responsible for Dunedin up to this time, warned the new arrivals in his Gallic way about the shortage of diocesan funds. 'I am tight,' he said pointing to himself. 'You are tight,' he told the bishop. And finally, pointing to the row of Dominican Sisters, 'We are all tight.'[2]

Moran was horrified at the rawness of his diocese. His first pastoral letter shocked his flock and gave notice that the new regime would be harsh and disciplined: '[How] deplorable is the state of religion here . . . the information given us in Europe as to the resources of this diocese and the preparation made for our coming was most incorrect . . . [This] diocese is [also] almost entirely destitute of the necessities of Divine Worship, such as altars, vestments, chalices and suitable altar ornaments . . .' To meet these challenges, the bishop would require 'a long sustained and generous effort and sacrifices of no small magnitude'.[3]

Rather unfairly Moran blamed the Marists for the circumstances he had inherited, overlooking the missionary nature of their station, their limited resources and the rapid and unforeseen population growth that had followed the gold rushes in the years immediately prior to his accession. The new bishop was determined, however, to impose ecclesiastical organisation on his frontier province; and he expected his priests, religious and

Hail glorious Saint Patrick,
Dear Saint of our isle!
On us thy poor children
Bestow a sweet smile.
And now thou art high
In thy mansions above,
On Erin's green valleys
Look down in thy love.

Saint Dominic's Priory, the 'concrete Gothic' convent and school designed by Francis Petre and built with funds raised by Bishop Moran. Work began on the site in 1877, six years after the Irish Dominican nuns arrived in Dunedin and had to be accommodated in the old Robin Hood Hotel.
~ *Dunedin Diocese*

laity to make sacrifices to that end, as he himself would. On the whole, he got the co-operation for which he asked.

By the time of Moran's death in 1895 the Dunedin Diocese had thirty-nine churches in fifteen parishes and twenty-nine Catholic schools. The number of Catholics was around 20,000 and they were served by twenty-two priests and eighty-seven religious. The bishop had brought in more Dominican Sisters, more Irish secular priests, and first Jesuits and then Christian Brothers to staff schools for boys. (The Jesuits stayed only ten years.) In 1873 he founded the weekly Catholic newspaper the *Tablet* and was its first editor. He stood for Parliament against the popular local member William Larnach in 1883. He built a fine stone cathedral, designed by Francis Petre, which opened in 1886 in the presence of his namesake Patrick Francis Moran, Cardinal Archbishop of Sydney. And he found time to act as administrator of the Wellington Diocese from 1872 to 1874, and of the Auckland Diocese from 1876 to 1879. In all of these tasks he was prodigiously energetic, relentlessly efficient and humourless.

The major way in which Bishop Moran came to the attention of the wider community, however, was as a polemicist on behalf of Irish Catholics. He berated the provincial and national governments for not supporting Catholic schools out of public funding (Catholics, he argued, paid taxes; they should not have to pay a second time to have their children educated). Catholics who sent their children to State schools in places where Catholic schools were available would be refused the sacraments and Christian burial. It was largely to dramatise the education issue that Moran founded the *Tablet* and stood (unsuccessfully) for Parliament. He vigorously opposed the 1877 Education Act, which made primary education in New Zealand 'free, compulsory and secular'; the bishop viewed it as part of a liberal-humanist conspiracy to de-Christianise the nation. A country that had for nearly forty years grown accustomed to genial Catholic bishops co-operating with civil authorities found Moran's opinions and tactics shocking.

The Bishop of Dunedin argued also, in public and in the privacy of Church 'official channels', that the predominantly Irish-Catholic population in New Zealand should be served by Irish bishops and priests. He was furious when Bishop Croke in Auckland was succeeded by at first a Dutch bishop (Steins) and then an English bishop (John Edmund Luck, from 1882). He was even more upset when the Wellington Diocese was given to Francis Redwood, whom Moran insisted on referring to as 'English' — though Redwood had left Staffordshire at the age of three. The most acrimonious controversy fanned by the Dunedin bishop, however, was that surrounding the appointment in 1887 of John Joseph

The traditional Gaelic greeting *cead mille failthe* ('a hundred thousand welcomes') reflects the presence of a large Irish-Catholic population in Greymouth in the late nineteenth century. The celebration, which may have been for visiting Irish politicians, took place outside Revington's Hotel.
~ *Alexander Turnbull Library*

Catholic funeral in Greymouth, also late nineteenth century. It was customary at this time for mourners ~ preceded by altar boys ~ to follow the cortège from the church to the cemetery.
~ Canterbury University

Grimes, an English Marist, to the new diocese of Christchurch. Moran refused to attend Grimes's installation as bishop, just as he refused the same year, as senior bishop, to invest Francis Redwood with the pallium, which would make the younger man Archbishop and Metropolitan of New Zealand — Moran believed that these titles should have gone to him.

At the time of the debate over Grimes's appointment and that of Redwood as Metropolitan, the *Tablet* revealed what it — and Moran — believed was going on: influential aristocratic English Catholics were seeking 'the eradication of all Irish characteristics from our Catholic population . . . Is it not enough that our people have been driven from the homes of their fathers by these people and their cruel legislation? . . . [Should they] be permitted to pursue us to the end of the earth in their efforts to cast reproach on us, and to continue to press the heel of tyranny and slander on our necks.'[4] This was paranoid Irish nonsense of a kind to which Moran was prone.

In spite of his penchant for conflict and controversy and his occasional displays of petulance, however, Patrick Moran was a great bishop who performed near-miracles of organisation in his diocese. He also ensured that the issue of religious education was publicly debated, even if the result he sought was not achieved by the Church in New Zealand for another 100 years. Ernest Simmons said of his episcopate:

'His home being right in the centre of the city, he [became] a familiar figure to the majority of the people of Dunedin, respected for his learning and his formidable debating skill by the university people, admired for his kindness to the poor and the lowly, consulted by many on the affairs of the city as well as the Church. He was always a man of plain and direct speech, speaking his mind honestly, and this was a characteristic which rather endeared him to the predominantly Scottish people of Otago. It was especially during [the] last years of his life that many of his former and current opponents in the education debate became his firm friends.'[5]

A coffin waits in Saint Mary's Church, Nelson, for a requiem Mass. The custom was that families would gather in the church the night before the funeral for the recitation of the rosary in the presence of the deceased.
~ Alexander Turnbull Library

❖

Some might have expected that, with Moran's death, the Irish profile of the New Zealand Catholic Church would fade. There were, for a brief time, no Irish bishops in the country. But that fact on its own is misleading. There were still Irish priests, nuns and brothers, and above all a laity who were largely Irish or of Irish descent. Irish issues still dominated the weekly *Tablet*. And Moran's successor in Dunedin in 1896, Michael Verdon, though English-born, was Irish — Maynooth-educated, nephew of Cardinal Cullen of Dublin and cousin of Cardinal Moran of Sydney. Bishop Grimes in Christchurch would be succeeded by Matthew Brodie, a New Zealand-Irish priest and first New Zealand-born bishop. And Auckland would again have an Irish bishop in Henry Cleary, who would succeed George Lenihan in 1910.

Even Francis Redwood of Wellington, Moran's *bête noire*, had considerable sympathy for the Irish and for the cause of Irish independence. In spite of his being born in Stafford his formative childhood years had been spent in New Zealand, his secondary education gained in France, and his early teaching and pastoral experience and his ordination had taken place in Ireland. Redwood had been ideally prepared to draw together all the threads of New Zealand's Catholic heritage. Like Moran, he transformed his diocese from a missionary domain into a modern ecclesiastical unit; unlike Moran, he sought to integrate the Catholic Church into the mainstream of New Zealand life and was a conciliator of some skill rather than a confrontationist. At the beginning of his

long episcopate in 1874 he was reputed to be the youngest bishop in the world; at the end of it, sixty-one years later, he was the oldest.

In 1874 Redwood was 'a handsome, solid, brown-bearded man of thirty-five with a singularly open and pleasant face . . . He was a fine speaker, had a great warmth of personality and could take it for granted that he was well accepted by any company he was in. Literature and music were his private enjoyments. Yet he was essentially a simple man who enjoyed meeting people and talking to them.'[6]

Redwood spent a good deal of time in the early years of his episcopate visiting and preaching missions in the outlying parishes of his diocese — something Viard in his later years had been unwilling or unable to do. The conditions of travel he described were those that any priest would have to contend with in rural areas. Of Taranaki in 1876, for example, Redwood wrote:

'Imagine the consequent state of the track — not road — converted by driven cattle into a quagmire up to the horse's knees,

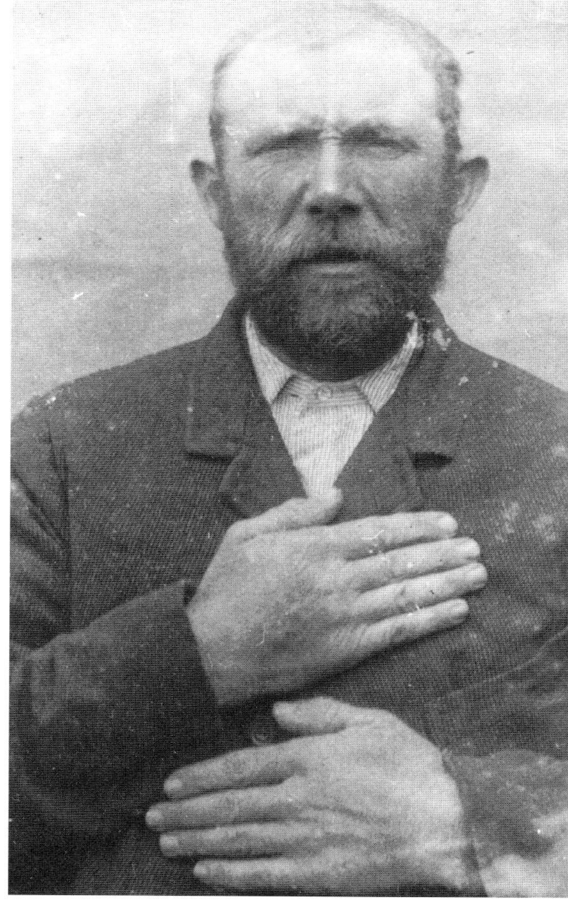

Itinerant uneducated labourers, of the kind referred to pejoratively as 'Bog Irish'. Both these men, born Catholic in Ireland, were arrested for criminal offences. The one on the left was still Catholic in 1889; the other, in spite of an apparently pious pose, gave his religion as 'agnostic'. Both photographs are from police files.
~ National Archives

nay, his very nostrils, when he stumbled, as he was apt to do, against the tangled hidden roots . . . Our horses [were] mud-coloured and ourselves bespattered from head to foot with mire. By a side street we reached the [New Plymouth] presbytery, avoiding public gaze. As we were bound on the Day of Obligation to hear Mass, I stole into the choir gallery out of the way. But, it appears, I scared the singers who never came, and so we had a low Mass . . . Neither [Father Hennebery] nor I had any church vesture to put on. He wanted his missionary cross and his cassock and I my robes. The silly man in charge of our bags had left them in the forest . . .'[7]

These were the kinds of conditions Patrick Moran had complained about when he reached Otago; Francis Redwood, by contrast, relished them. It was a mark of how much more a New Zealander he was than some of his brother bishops. The same harsh conditions were encountered daily by Catholic settlers outside the main centres. And, as a consequence of the immigration schemes initiated by Julius Vogel, these immigrants by the 1870s and 1880s included Catholics from countries and cultures other than England and Ireland: German-speaking Bohemians who settled in Puhoi north of Auckland and around Ohaupo; displaced Poles who settled parts of Taranaki, the Wairarapa, the Taieri Plain and Marshlands (on the outskirts of Christchurch); 'Austrians', who were in fact Croatians from the coast of Dalmatia, who began working in the Northland gumfields and then shifted into farming and horticulture; and Italians who went to the West Coast of the South Island, the Wairarapa, and (increasingly from the late nineteenth century) to fishing communities on the shore of Cook Strait. Their presence in New Zealand reflected the international character of Catholicism and went some small way towards breaking down the xenophobia which many Pakeha New Zealanders felt towards non-British immigrants.

Taranaki, Wairarapa, the Manawatu and Hawke's Bay were all organised into parish units as they were further opened up for settlement and development in the first decade of Redwood's episcopate. Other new parishes were established in Canterbury and Westland, still part of Wellington until the foundation of the Christchurch diocese in 1887.

In Wellington city in 1876 Redwood brought in the Marist Brothers of the Schools, the teaching order which had — at Rome's insistence — separated itself from the Society of Mary in 1852, to run primary schools for boys. The inaugural group was made up of two Frenchmen, one Irishman and an Englishman. The brothers who followed were largely Irish and Continental Europeans who came to New Zealand via Australia. In 1885 Redwood fulfilled one of his major ambitions by opening Saint Patrick's College in

Foundation staff at Saint Patrick's College, Wellington, in 1885, fresh from Mother Ireland. From left ~ Fathers James Goggan, Thomas Devoy, Felix Watters (rector) and Nicholas Carolan.
~ Saint Patrick's College

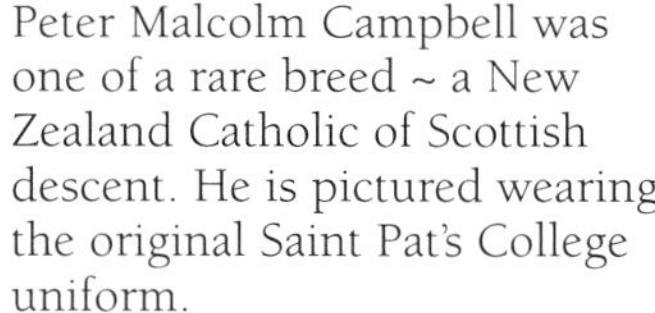

Peter Malcolm Campbell was one of a rare breed ~ a New Zealand Catholic of Scottish descent. He is pictured wearing the original Saint Pat's College uniform.
~ L. M. Campbell

Wellington, which was only the second Catholic secondary boarding school for boys since the establishment of Pompallier's college for Maori students in Auckland (the intervening one had been 'the Academy' in Ahaura on the West Coast, which operated from 1875 to 1883).

The new Wellington college was staffed largely by Irish Marists from Dundalk. The Rector was Father Felix Watters, whose Jesuit brother was president of University College in Dublin when James Joyce was a student there. The prospectus noted that 'as the vast majority of Catholic youths in the colony are sons of Erin, the college is named after the great apostle of Ireland [and] is intended to provide . . . the advantages of the great public schools of Europe.'[8] Not even Bishop Moran could quibble at that: it was a strong riposte to his accusation that Redwood was determined to anglicise the Church in New Zealand.

Saint Pat's became the country's leading Catholic college. Astonishingly, Redwood lived long enough to open a matching school in 1931, Saint Patrick's College at Silverstream in the Hutt Valley, which took over the boarding establishment.

The Stoke Industrial School near Nelson had a less happy history. Nelson remained part of Wellington after the Christchurch diocese had been peeled off. Father Garin had established an orphanage there in 1874 but this was turned into an industrial school in 1881. A branch opened at Stoke in 1886 and was staffed by Marist Brothers from 1890. Ten years later a snap inspection by the Nelson Charitable Aid Board and a subsequent investigation by a Royal Commission found serious fault with the school. The use of corporal punishment was judged to be excessive, washing and bathing facilities inadequate. Food and clothing were deemed sufficient but greater variety was called for. Allegations of sexual abuse were not sustained, though this may have been a consequence of an unwillingness to take the word of 'problem children' over that of adult members of a religious order. (Later experience suggests that some institutions were inclined to dismiss

Rugby was a major part of the culture of Catholic boys secondary schools. This Saint Patrick's Wellington team played on the day the school opened. It includes three nephews of Archbishop Redwood and a future archbishop, Thomas O'Shea (standing far left). The coach is the Irish rector, Dr Watters.
~ *Marist Archives*

The washroom in the Stoke Orphanage, Nelson, in 1909 ~ almost a decade after the Marist Brothers had handed the institution over to lay staff.
~ *Nelson Provincial Museum*

such allegations and protect alleged offenders; it was not until the 1990s that adequate protocols were developed for dealing with accusations of sexual assault.) The Marist Brothers handed the Stoke school back to the diocese. It was administered by lay staff until its closure in 1918.[9]

Over this period the Wellington Maori mission enjoyed a spectacular revival. Father François Melu reopened the Pukekaraka station at Otaki and from there had churches built at Kauangaroa, Poroutawhao, Mangamaunu, Oahau, Awahuri and Paraparaumu. He was joined there in the 1890s by Father François Delach, who left a deep impression on all who met him and heard him preach. Both priests were also responsible for Maori communities in Marlborough and Canterbury. Other Marists returned to the Whanganui River communities in the 1880s. Father Christophe Soulas went to Hiruharama (Jerusalem) in 1883, and he took with him Father Delphin Moreau, now old and ailing and in the last year of his life, two sisters of Saint Joseph of Nazareth (a congregation that had separated from Mother Mary MacKillop's Sisters of Saint Joseph of the Sacred Heart in 1876 and established a convent at Wanganui in 1880), and Suzanne Aubert, who would establish a church, a convent, an orchard and a new religious order there.

Now forty-eight years of age, Aubert had 'greatly matured and developed; she . . . had twenty years of experience with the Maoris, spoke their language, understood them very well and had taught

Boarders at the six-year-old Blessed Peter Chanel Convent School at Pukekaraka, Otaki, in 1900. Most of the day pupils were local Maori. The Sisters of Saint Joseph of Nazareth are Sister Veronica Lee (left) and Sister Margaret-Mary Jillett.
~ *Marist Archives*

A class at the Marist Brothers' primary school in Boulcott Street, Wellington, 1890s. The teacher on the right wearing the order's customary French clerical collar is Brother Mark. This school, the brothers' first in Wellington, moved subsequently to Thorndon.
~ *Pat Lawlor Collection*

Suzanne Aubert in her Daughters of Our Lady of Compassion habit poses with her 'foundlings' at Jerusalem on the Whanganui River, 1898. A year later she would move the headquarters of her religious order and work to Wellington.
~ Sisters of Compassion Archive

A selection of Mother Aubert's patent medicines, marketed by Sharland's in the late nineteenth century. Wanena was in effect an antibiotic preparation to prevent the infection of cuts and wounds. Other herbal remedies were on offer for rheumatism, heartburn, indigestion, influenza, whooping cough and asthma.
~ Sisters of Compassion Archive

herself the skills of a back-country nurse . . . [But] some characteristics were not only still present but greatly intensified — her deep faith, her dedication to the Maori people, her steely determination in the face of difficulties. The Sisters of Saint Joseph withdrew from the Jerusalem venture after a year and Suzanne Aubert took over responsibility for the school, bringing into existence a new order . . .'[10]

It was intended that this new religious congregation would be linked to the Society of Mary, with whom Suzanne Aubert had been working in close harmony since 1871. But the society decided in 1892 that the spirit of Aubert's new congregation was different from that of Marist groups. So Redwood re-christened it 'the Daughters of Our Lady of Compassion'. These nuns, under Aubert's charismatic leadership, would branch out into a variety of welfare work, initially with Maori children and 'foundlings'. They received papal approval in 1917 and remain the only surviving religious congregation founded in New Zealand.

Other Redwood initiatives contributed to the indigenisation of New Zealand clergy. Saint Patrick's College in Wellington produced 126 priests between the time of its foundation and the Archbishop's death. Of these, 103 became Marists. Redwood also helped the Marists establish their own seminary at Meeanee in 1890, which was shifted to Mount Saint Mary's, Greenmeadows, in 1911. One of the foundation students was Thomas O'Shea,

First Communion Group at Otaki, 1898, with Fathers Thomas O'Shea and François Delach. The man in front is believed to be catechist and bell-ringer Hakaraia Rangikura, who was associated with the Pukekaraka mission from 1850 to 1916.
~ *Marist Archives*

The Marist seminary in Meeanee, opened in 1890. Four years later the staff was made up of (standing, from left) Fathers David Kennedy and Thomas O'Shea, and (sitting, from left) Fathers Nicolas Binsfeld, Placide Hualt, Jean Goutenoire and François Yardin. David Kennedy was the first New Zealand-born Marist. In addition to his qualifications in theology and philosophy he had a degree in mathematics and science. His photographs of Halley's Comet taken from his observatory at Meeanee in 1910 were admired and published around the world. The seminary shifted to neighbouring Mount Saint Mary's, Greenmeadows, in 1911.
~ Marist Archives

who would be Redwood's successor as Archbishop of Wellington. In 1899 the New Zealand bishops decided to fund a national seminary for training secular priests. Its establishment was entrusted to Bishop Verdon of Dunedin, who had previously been vice-rector of the Irish College in Rome and rector of the Manly Seminary in Sydney. Holy Cross College opened in Mosgiel in 1900. There was now no further need for New Zealand priests to train in Australia, which they had been required to do since the closure of Pompallier's seminary. Henceforth almost all New Zealand-born priests would be educated at either Mosgiel or — in the case of Marists — at first Meeanee and then Greenmeadows, with especially promising candidates completing their studies in Rome.

One of Redwood's few disappointing ventures was an attempt to set up a Catholic paper in opposition to what he viewed as the intemperate voice of the *Tablet*. His *Catholic Times* first appeared in January 1888. It 'favoured Irish self-government, insisted that Catholics were loyal New Zealanders and covered religious and social issues'.[11] Redwood had less success than Moran finding suitable editors. His first, a Mr Meale, 'was dismissed for drunkenness, looseness in accounting for money and debts which brought about his imprisonment'.[12] The paper closed in 1894.

Holy Cross College, Mosgiel, which opened in 1900 as a national seminary for diocesan priests under Bishop Michael Verdon's supervision. Originally the property had been the home of Arthur Burns, stalwart Otago Presbyterian and great-nephew of the poet Robbie Burns.
~ Marist Archives

Professorial staff at Holy Cross College in 1906 ~ (from left) Fathers J. Delaney, J. M. Liston, Bishop Verdon, Fathers D. Buckley and M. Ryan.
~ Holy Cross College

Among inaugural candidates for the priesthood at Mosgiel ~ (from left) P. Minogue, J. Griffin, J. McNamee and J. H. Parker.
~ *Holy Cross College*

As his episcopate advanced and more Catholic laity became established in business and commercial life, Redwood received better advice on financial matters than had previously been available to him and more donations of money and land for the diocese. One such confidant was Martin Kennedy, an Irishman who had come to New Zealand to work the West Coast goldfields. He did well in Greymouth, becoming owner of a coal mine and a fleet of colliers. He was elected to Parliament in 1876 (but resigned two years later).

In 1889 Kennedy moved to Wellington where, in addition to business activities — which included a directorship of the Bank of New Zealand — he became deeply involved in Church affairs. He had already helped introduce to New Zealand the Hibernian Catholic Benefit Society — a kind of Catholic Masonic group — in Greymouth in 1869. He remained involved in the society in Wellington and took a leading role in the charitable work of the Saint Vincent de Paul Society. He donated land for Marist Brothers schools in Thorndon and Newtown, and he funded scholarships to Saint Patrick's College. As a supporter of Irish Home Rule, Kennedy organised visits to New Zealand of advocates of that cause. He was typical of that first generation of Irish Catholics 'who arrived in New Zealand with little capital, limited vocational skills and few social advantages, yet were able to prosper and to achieve a substantial measure of public eminence'.[13]

Martin Kennedy, born in County Tipperary in the 1830s, arrived in Otago in 1861 a penurious would-be goldminer. A decade later he had accumulated sufficient capital to buy into the Brunnerton Colliery on the West Coast. He moved to Wellington in 1889 and devoted the rest of his life to business interests and Catholic affairs. He had introduced the Hibernians to New Zealand in 1869 and in the capital was prominent in the Saint Vincent de Paul Society. He died wealthy and respected in 1916.
~ Alexander Turnbull Library

The second generation of such migrants was represented by the likes of Patrick Joseph O'Regan, who lifted himself out of the working class on the Coast and into the professions in the capital (O'Regan becoming a lawyer and, eventually, a Judge of the Arbitration Court). Kennedy and O'Regan were among those who, with Redwood, 'helped to bring the Catholic Church into the main-stream of New Zealand life'.[14]

Not wholly into the mainstream, however. It was in the late nineteenth century that sodalities such as the Children of Mary were introduced into New Zealand parishes. These were associations of laity who met to perform spiritual exercises under the eye of a director, usually the parish priest. Their aims were partly to sanctify individuals, partly to do good works, and partly to provide a Catholic social life away from the temptations of secular society. A Children of Mary manual, for example, warned against the reading of 'all romances, in which are mingled intrigues more or less capable of exciting the passions'. Even more dangerous were 'songs of the same nature, the melody and harmony of which render them more seductive'.[15]

Simmons has commented that the sodalities 'strengthened the links between family and Church, reinforcing the work of the parish Mass, priestly visitation and Catholic school . . . [Catholics] gradually developed [their] own institutions parallel to those of the general community . . . Catholic sports clubs, dances, card evenings . . .'[16] And the ultimate aim of most such clubs was to make it more likely that good Catholic boys married good Catholic girls.

The city of Wellington became even more important as the centre of government after abolition of the provinces in 1876. This fact meant that, at least in the later years of the nineteenth century, it was most often Redwood who liaised with Catholic parliamentarians on issues and legislation in which the Church had a particular interest. He had meetings with Catholic cabinet minister John Sheehan, for example, about the 1877 Education

James and Mary Mullins (née Kelleher) were both born in Ireland but married in Wairoa. They had twelve children. James worked as a road builder in Te Mapara, Te Kuiti and Auckland, and in each community they became involved in parish fund raising. Mary died in Wairoa in 1938 after delivering a bowl of soup to a sick neighbour; James in 1941.
~ *E. P. O'Leary*

Con O'Leary of Wanganui was a typical Irish-Catholic immigrant of the nineteenth century. Born in County Cork in 1861, he came to New Zealand in 1885 at the suggestion of his older brother, Monsignor Patrick O'Leary of Lawrence. Con spent the rest of his working life in New Zealand Railways and was Inspector of Permanent Way at his retirement. He was a life member of the Hibernians and founded the Saint Vincent de Paul Society in Wanganui.
He married Julia McMahon from County Kerry and they had two sons and three daughters.
He died in 1943.
~ E. P. O'Leary

Act (fruitless ones, given that Sheehan turned out to be a supporter of the bill); and, from the 1890s, Redwood had both social contact and professional discussions with Joseph Ward — not the Joseph Ward who was his brother-in-law, although he too served briefly in Parliament, but Joseph George Ward, the Southland politician and later second Catholic Prime Minister of New Zealand, whose ministerial career extended over an extraordinary thirty-nine years. One of Ward's prominent Liberal colleagues, the Maori cabinet minister James Carroll, was also Catholic but — according to one historian — 'never worked at it'.[17] Hugh Poland, for twenty years Catholic MP for Ohinemuri, never reached cabinet; but he

Archbishop Francis Redwood ~ once the youngest bishop in the world; eventually the oldest. Here he arrives at the Basin Reserve in Wellington for celebrations to mark his episcopal diamond jubilee. Appropriately, he is met by an honour guard of Hibernians.
~ Marist Archives

was a fierce advocate for his constituency of Coromandel miners and a trusted adviser to Redwood on matters affecting Catholic workers.

Because of the length of his episcopate and his geniality to all, the citizens of Wellington came to regard Archbishop Redwood as a kind of civic institution in his own right. He was admired and liked in a non-sectarian way. The regularity of his routine meant that people always knew when and how to see him.

In the years of his prime, 'he would normally rise at exactly 5 am . . . and begin the day with meditation and other prayers to aid his Mass at 7 am in his house chapel. After breakfast at 8 am he would go to his office to recite the Church's office for the day. Then he answered letters and attended to whatever other business there was. For those who wrote to him for permission to do something he would turn up the bottom left-hand corner of their letter and reply briefly before signing and sealing it. At 10 am he would see anyone who wanted to see him — these appointments were always brief. Following this he would put on his bell-topper, having taken from it the letters placed ready for posting. From his house in Hill Street he would walk down Lambton Quay to the Post Office. There he would post his letters and collect the mail before proceeding up Boulcott Street to the Terrace. There he usually met Rabbi van Stavern, who was also a regular walker, and the two men, Christian and Jew, would converse with each other before parting to return to their respective homes.

'After returning from his walk he would relax with some reading until midday when he would say the Angelus and prepare the office of Matins and Lauds for the next day. At 12.30 he had dinner. In later years, on days that he did not take a walk, he liked to be driven by one of his priests around the waterfront, or to see his niece Mother Bernard at Seatoun. At 5 pm he would say his vespers before tea at 6 pm. After this he conversed with his fellow priests before beginning his violin practice at 7 pm [he had a Stradivarius]. That was followed by night prayer, and supper at 9 pm before retiring to bed. At mealtimes Redwood liked to sit at the head of the table, and would always carve the meat. Unlike some bishops of the day, he saw meals as a time for fraternising with his fellow priests rather than a time of silence.'[18]

By 1900 Redwood's diocese had twenty-six parishes, seventy-nine churches, forty Marist priests, fourteen secular, thirty-four brothers, 236 nuns, nine secondary schools, twenty-eight primary schools and four orphanages. With 26,000 Catholics it was slightly larger than the other three, all of which had between 20,000 and 25,000 Church members. Over the coming decades, however,

Catechism class in Wairoa, about 1912. The instructing priest may be Father Celestin Lacroix. In areas without Catholic schools it was common practice for Catholic children to be released from school for religious instruction, or to receive it outside school hours.
~ *E. P. O'Leary*

First communicants, Invercargill, 1911, with parish priest Dean V. F. Burke.
~ *Dunedin Diocese*

growth would be uneven. Auckland and Wellington would expand at a faster rate (37,000 and 54,000 Catholics respectively by 1914, for example); Christchurch would develop more slowly; and Dunedin scarcely at all. And it was this disproportionate pattern of development that would eventually lead to the creation in 1980 of two further dioceses, Hamilton and Palmerston North, trimmed off Auckland and Wellington respectively.

In Christchurch, the episcopate of John Joseph Grimes did not prosper to the same extent as that of his Wellington Marist confrère. Grimes was a cockney born in Spitalfields who studied with the Marists in France and Ireland. He was ordained in Dublin in 1869 and came to New Zealand in 1888 after teaching in the United States and England. On his arrival he walked straight into major conflict between the Irish secular priests in his new diocese and the Marists, who were slightly in the majority.

This division was a consequence of the fact that Marists had founded the New Zealand Catholic mission but were unable to staff it on their own. Indeed, it had never been their intention that they should do so. While they had been withdrawn from Auckland and not invited back to Moran's Dunedin, they remained a strong presence in Wellington and Christchurch, which they regarded as being in their gift, because the founding documents of both dioceses had specified that Marists were to develop them. Hence they expected the bishops there to be Marists. This *was* so in Wellington (which had a Marist archbishop in the person of Thomas O'Shea until 1954); and it was initially so in Christchurch. But the predominantly Irish secular priests in Christchurch disliked the collegiality of the religious order and felt that the Marists were being given the most affluent parishes as a result of episcopal favour. The seculars also shared Bishop Moran's view that a largely Irish flock needed an Irish bishop and clergy, preferably drawn from secular ranks. They expressed hostility to Grimes's appointment. In these circumstances, according to one source, 'some of the clergy took advantage of the disorder in Christchurch and turned to drink and card playing until caught by Ginaty', the Marist rector of Christchurch.[19]

On the whole, though, the ready-made diocese Grimes inherited from Redwood's stewardship was in good shape. It had nineteen parishes and a generous supply of priests, brothers, nuns and schools. Religious orders working there included the Sisters of Our Lady of the Missions in Christchurch itself, the Sisters of Mercy (in Hokitika since 1878 and Greymouth since 1882), and the Sisters of the Sacred Heart in Timaru (who would subsequently open boarding schools in Wellington and Auckland). The Marist Brothers ran a boys school in Christchurch and the Sisters of the

Saint Mary's Church, Hokitika, built over fourteen years, monumentalises the piety of the Catholic Irish of the West Coast in the late nineteenth and early twentieth century. According to one art historian, such buildings represented 'a huge expression of faith and affirmation of presence in the community'.
~ *Peter Quinn*

By the early 1900s New Zealand Catholic families were beginning to make contributions, in some cases major ones, to religious orders. Of these seven daughters of Hughie Brosnahan, a South Canterbury publican, three joined the Sisters of Saint Joseph of the Sacred Heart ~ Sisters Rita, Fergus and Lucian. Three others ~ Emma, Mary and Nora ~ produced daughters who became nuns. The seventh, Debbie (second from right) remained unmarried. The photograph was taken in about 1913.
~ Peg Cadigan

Good Shepherd looked after delinquent girls there.

The Sisters of Saint Joseph of the Sacred Heart, founded in Australia by the formidable Mother Mary MacKillop, opened a convent at Temuka in 1883, the first of ten houses the order would establish in New Zealand before the close of the nineteenth century. On two of her four visits to New Zealand, in 1894 and 1897, Mother Mary stayed at the Temuka convent. These visits, and others to Arrowtown, Paeroa, Rotorua and Auckland, assumed larger significance a century later when the Josephite founder was beatified by Pope John Paul II, thus raising the prospect that Mother Mary might come to be recognised as the first canonised saint to visit New Zealand (if there was a competitor for this honour in the minds of the Faithful, it would be Suzanne Aubert, another courageous and inspirational woman ahead of her time who would also come to be regarded as a candidate for canonisation).[20]

The disposition of Christchurch parishes and religious staff had changed little by 1900. This was probably a reflection of the fact that its fifty-five priests, 150 nuns and thirteen brothers were about the right complement for its population of around 23,000 Catholics. Christchurch had ended its phase of rapid growth. The disproportionate number of nuns to brothers was explained by a factor that applied in all dioceses at this time: sisters taught boys and girls at primary level, whereas secondary-aged boys were taught by brothers only: initially Marists, much later Christian Brothers too (who had been invited to the diocese in 1877 but did not begin teaching there until 1961). It was assumed nationally, among clergy, religious and laity, that the resources of the Church should be focused primarily on providing an alternative school system; and that religious teachers — for whom teaching was a vocation within the Church and who required only minimum salaries — were the best people to staff such a system. This view would not be seriously challenged until the 1960s.

Bishop Grimes did take one startling initiative. He decided that, like his fellow bishops, he needed a cathedral and he engaged the Catholic architect Francis William Petre (son of Henry Petre of Wellington), who had already designed Saint Dominic's priory and Saint Joseph's cathedral in Dunedin, and striking churches for the towns of Oamaru and Invercargill. Grimes's basilica-style building, the Cathedral of the Blessed Sacrament, outstripped all of its predecessors in size, quantity of building materials and grandeur of design. It was opened in 1905 at a cost of £52,000.

Bishop John Joseph Grimes of Christchurch and Father Theophile Le Menant des Chesnais pose with contractors responsible for moving the diocese's pro-cathedral prior to beginning work on the massive Cathedral of the Blessed Sacrament. The laymen are John Collins, Richard Harman and Andrew Swanston.
~ Alexander Turnbull Library

A bevy of prelates gathered for Bishop Grimes's day of triumph ~ the opening of his cathedral on 12 February 1905. Talking to his lordship in the centre of the photograph are the Governor Lord Plunkett and his wife. Prime Minister Richard Seddon stands behind the bishop's left shoulder, and Bishop George Lenihan of Auckland is to the right. The Catholic deputy-Prime Minister, Joseph Ward, talks to Archbishop Carr of Melbourne at the end of the front row of dignitaries. Other Australasian bishops present are Reville, Dunne and Verdon. ~ *Christchurch Diocese*

Some of the bishop's priests and laity viewed it as a building that would honour God and grace the city; others spoke of it as an unpardonable extravagance, particularly when cost overruns came to light. There was no doubt, though, that its completion gave New Zealand one of its finest examples of church architecture.[21]

Oddly, there was one part of Grimes's diocese which had a small Catholic population that had never been visited by a bishop or a priest. This was the Chatham Islands, 870 km to the east of the mainland. Before the islands were annexed by New Zealand in 1842, the Marist superior Jean-Claude Colin had suggested that a central college for the Oceania mission be established there; but this plan had not been pursued. Catholics had lived on the islands from as early as the 1830s and had long hoped for a visit from a priest. Grimes himself decided to go there in 1896 but was then persuaded that his health was not up to the rigours of the journey (a three-day trip from Lyttelton, a further sea voyage

The Chatham Islands, off the east coast of the South Island, remained New Zealand's ~ and the Catholic Church's ~ last frontier. An absence of roads, vehicles, electricity and other amenities ensured that life on the Chathams was reminiscent of pioneering days on the mainland. Here Father John Sarsfield O'Brien (right), first priest appointed to the islands, escorts Bishop Matthew Brodie on a pastoral visit in 1935.
~ V. McSweeney

Father J. McGuire, relieving priest on the Chathams in 1938, holds the bridle of his transport and the hand of a young parishioner.
~ V. McSweeney

between Chatham and Pitt Islands, and the need to ride horseback on barely formed tracks).

The bishop sent instead James Foley, a forty-nine-year-old Marist, in August 1896. And Father Foley confirmed everybody's fears that the islands were dangerous. On Chatham Island the priest fell twice from his horse, each time sustaining injuries that required convalescence (one of the islanders who took him in and put him to bed was a German Moravian missioner, J. G. Engst). Then, as Foley was about to leave in October, his Maori bearers accidentally tipped him out of a litter across the thwarts of a surf boat and fractured his ribs. Back in Christchurch Father Foley needed months of further convalescence before he was fit to work again. The Church did not risk sending more priests to the Chathams for another nineteen years. The loyal Catholic flock there were grateful for the visit, however, and for the baptisms, marriages and Masses that resulted. They wrote a moving address to Father Foley on the occasion of his departure and commiserated with him over his accidents.[22]

For the five years that Auckland was without a bishop in the 1870s and in the period following Bishop Steins's death in 1881 the diocese was overseen by Bishop Moran from Dunedin. On a day-to-day basis, however, it was capably administered by the Vicar General, an English secular priest named Henry Fynes. In this period new churches opened in Waikato (Ohaupo, Taupiri, Hamilton, Cambridge and Kihikihi) and old ones were renovated (Alexandra, Ngaruawahia and Rangiaowhia). The first resident priest was appointed to Gisborne, and Puhoi, site of the Bohemian settlement, became a parish in its own right.

The weakness in Fynes's administration, and in Moran's, was a lack of concern for Maori people who had been the focus of interest for the Church's original New Zealand mission. This was to some extent compensated for by James McDonald's assuming responsibility for northern Maori after 1880. For the next decade, based first at Maketu and subsequently at Purakau, he made prodigious journeys on horseback and foot through the outback Maori communities. It was a job that had been carried out four decades earlier by a team of priests. It was far too much for one middle-aged man, no matter how dedicated.

By this time Maketanara, as McDonald was called, looked like an Old Testament prophet: a wraith-like figure with long white hair and beard, he would arrive in a village with his Maori attendants, say Mass, baptise new babies, hear Confessions, and then refuse to leave until the locals had erected (or repaired) their raupo chapel. His pronouncements became progressively more oracular and then obscure, and towards the end of his life he seems to have been suffering from premature senility. But his flock respected and loved him, and appear to have concluded that his illness was simply an indication of his proximity to Eternity. He was called with justification the 'Apostle of the Maori'. He died alone at Purakau in July 1890.

Father James McDonald with Maori altar boys, Whangaroa, November 1885.
~ Auckland Diocese

One curious thing McDonald discovered as he entered communities that had not seen a priest for a decade: the Faith had often been kept alive by the work of catechists such as Heremia Te Wake of Panguru. Heremia had been born about 1838, the year of Pompallier's arrival in the Hokianga. He had taken part in inter-tribal fighting in the 1860s and had at one point been imprisoned for murder.

Between 1873 and 1880, when the Church had abandoned what had been its first New Zealand pastorate in the Far North, Heremia led the prayers of the Mass on Sundays and Holy Days, baptised infants, instructed children and adults in the catechism and led prayers for the dead. He and his fellow catechists Re Te Tai and Nui Hare did much to keep Catholicism alive among the Rarawa people of the Hokianga, who had first heard of this religion from Thomas and Mary Poynton. Later Heremia cooperated with James McDonald, and with the Mill Hill priests

Mill Hill Maori missioner John Becker at Purakau with Northern Hokianga Catholic community leaders. From left ~ Nui Hare (Motukaraka), Re Te Tai (Waihou), Niheta Tukupoto Peita (Whakarapa), Heremia Te Wake (Te Karaka later Whakarapa), Toma Te Whiu (Waihou), Te Wau Peita (Whakarapa) and Rini Te Whiu (Waihou).
~ Auckland Diocese

Opposite
Father Martin Alink conducts an outdoor Mass at Hoe-o-Tainui in Waikato. Father Alink was a Mill Hill based at this time at Rotorua.
~ Auckland Diocese

Father Richard Bressers, who was working from the new Hokianga station at Rawene, conducts the funeral of one of the Te Tai family at Waihou in 1931.
~ Whina Cooper

who took over the Maori mission. He was also responsible for the building of Saint Peter's church in Panguru in 1883.

McDonald's successors, the Mill Hill Fathers, were brought to Auckland by Bishop John Luck. This order was actually called Saint Joseph's Foreign Missionary Society and had been founded at Mill Hill in London by Father — later Cardinal — Herbert Vaughan. Its first priests arrived in New Zealand in 1886: John Becker, a thirty-year-old German who would in time become as well known and respected (but not as loved) as Maketanara; and James Medan, a forty-five-year-old Englishman. They based themselves first at Matata and looked after Catholic Maori south of Auckland. After McDonald's death they and subsequent Mill Hill reinforcements took over the mission north of Auckland as well and Becker lived at Purakau.

The Mill Hills were to retain their Maori responsibilities in the Auckland Diocese for the best part of a century. Becker and the priests who arrived after him, largely German and Dutch, shared an advantage with their French Marist predecessors. They were expatriates. English-speaking clergy tended to be seen by Maori as New Zealanders first and priests second — and this was a factor in the withdrawal of priests from the Maori mission. The Mill Hills had no such ambivalence. They were priests ahead of any other role; and (some would say) they were Maori second,

IHS

because so many of them lived with and identified with their Maori congregations. Many of them became more proficient in the Maori language than in English. One of their lasting legacies in the North was the solid churches they built from the 1880s into the 1900s. Some, such as those left by the carpenter-priest Carl Kreijmborg, outlasted the communities in which they had originally stood.

Over the same period the Marists continued to be responsible for the Maori pastorate in the Wellington Diocese, although the conditions in which they lived and worked were seldom as harsh as those encountered by many of the Mill Hills. The heroes of the southern mission were men such as Christophe Soulas and Claude Cognet of the Whanganui region and François Melu and François

Father François Melu survived into the 1930s to give a new generation of priests the benefit of his more than fifty years' proselytising among Maori. Here he greets seven-foot-tall Father Arthur James McRae, later a monsignor and Vicar General of the Wellington Diocese and one of the major personalities among the leaders of the New Zealand Church until his death in 1964.
~ *Marist Archives*

Opposite
The church of Saint Cletus in Waihou, built in Spanish style by Father Carl Kreijmborg during the First World War. It was one of a dozen northern churches built by this German-Dutch priest, who died in a car accident in 1928.
~ *Michael King*

Interior of Saint Joseph's Church at Motuti, a small community on the northern side of Hokianga Harbour. This building was moved from Purakau by one of the Mill Hill builder priests, Father Carl Kreijmborg.
~ *Auckland Diocese*

Delach of Pukekaraka, Otaki. Delach's most effective mission came to a sudden and premature end, however. He believed deeply that Maori should enter the church as Maori and remain culturally Maori; and that the mixing of Maori and Pakeha ingredients in single parish units would not work.

This put him on a collision course with the Wellington co-adjutor, Bishop Thomas O'Shea, who described the Pukekawa religious hui organised by Delach and Melu as 'useless big meetings, which made a great show, but from which absolutely no benefit resulted'.[23] O'Shea transferred Delach from Otaki to Hawke's Bay; the demoralised Frenchman returned to France in 1917 and died there in 1949.

Father Jim Riordan, one of the most popular and best known of the Marist Maori missioners, pictured at a confirmation hui at Wairoa in 1943. His companion is Joe Brosnahan of Ngati Kahungunu, who had just been confirmed after a ten-day catechism camp at Takitimu Marae.
~ *Peg Cadigan*

Overleaf (p.130) ~ Te Uira Te Heuheu was a member of one of the most distinguished Maori Catholic families. Her father, Te Heuheu Tukino, was ariki of Ngati Tuwharetoa. Te Uira was educated by Sisters of Mercy at Saint Mary's Convent in Wellington and plucked from there into a taumau or arranged marriage with the Tainui kahui ariki (royal family).
She subsequently married a member of her own tribe. She was an immensely supportive patron of both Mill Hill and Marist Maori missioners in the Auckland and Wellington dioceses.
~ *Museum of New Zealand*

After Delach's departure the momentum of activity at Pukekaraka slowed to a halt; indeed the morale of the entire Wellington Maori mission was affected adversely. Eventually lost ground was made up by a later generation of non-French Marists, Jim Riordan, Gus Venning, Jim Durning and Frank Wall among them. They received loyal support from such rangatira Catholic families as the Te Heuheus, the Huras, the Marius and the Takarangis. But they were not always as well understood by their religious confrères.

To the Marists, though, would go the honour of training the first Maori Catholic priest, Wiremu Te Awhitu, ordained in 1944; and the first Maori Catholic bishop, Max Takuira Mariu, consecrated in 1988, was also a Marist.

A hui at Otaki in December 1904 to christen the new marae at Pukekaraka. Father François Delach is standing in front of the whare tapu, site of Father Jean-Baptiste Comte's first mission house. The totara cross on the summit of Pukekaraka is visible at right. A decade later Father Delach was withdrawn from Otaki in the wake of complaints that he devoted too much time to his Maori parishioners. The new coadjutor in Wellington, Thomas O'Shea, wanted Maori and Pakeha parishes combined. Father Delach returned to France in 1917 but lived until 1949, last survivor of the French Marist mission to the Maori.
~ Marist Archives

Other changes had taken place in Auckland in the course of John Luck's episcopate (1882–96). Luck's fellow Benedictine priests had made up about half of the diocese's clergy between 1880 and 1890, serving Catholic congregations north of Puhoi, in the Waikato and at Coromandel. They also built the imposing Saint Benedict's church in Newton in 1886. Luck invited the Marist Brothers into the diocese and they opened Sacred Heart School for boys in Ponsonby in 1885. The Sisters of Saint Joseph of the Sacred Heart began teaching at Newton in 1884, and the Sisters of the Missions in Hamilton in 1884 and Pukekohe in 1885. The Little Sisters of the Poor established a home for the indigent elderly in Ponsonby in 1888.

All of this represented considerable progress in extending the facilities of the diocese, particularly its schools. Bishop Luck was

A bishop at work ~ frail, saintly John Luck, an English Benedictine, presided over a period of growth in the Auckland diocese from 1882 to 1896. Here he works in his study in the new 'Bishop's Palace' in Ponsonby soon after its completion in 1894.
~ *Auckland Diocese*

While he preferred to wear his simple Benedictine habit at home Bishop Luck dressed in rather more episcopal fashion when he was on public display. In this instance he prepares to enter his carriage for a diocesan visitation in 1883.
Auckland Diocese

also to open a new and greatly enlarged Saint Patrick's Cathedral in 1894 and an imposing new Bishop's House in Ponsonby the same year. In spite of the fact that he initiated and presided over a period of major development, the bishop was viewed by his clergy and laity as a fragile and tentative figure. This may have been because the last ten years of his life were lived under the threat of death from heart disease. '[Those] ten years were both active and fruitful [however]. He was, by nature, a rather low-spirited man and his years in Auckland were saddened by a good deal of opposition — from his own Benedictines, from those of his subjects who mistrusted an Englishman, and from the rather vocal bigots among the Protestants. He was [never] a popular bishop, yet he did more than any other . . . to put the diocese on a sound footing and to give it the establishment needed for his work.'[24]

His successor in 1896, who was able to benefit from and to a large extent ride on the momentum generated by Luck, was the popular English parish priest of Ponsonby George Lenihan. According to the diocesan historian, he was 'a kindly man, cultivated and musical, but without much of the quality which makes a leader or an administrator'.[25] The diocese continued to function, however, as a result of the infrastructure already in place and the

Bishop Luck's successor, George Lenihan (nearest camera), may have been the first Catholic prelate in New Zealand to make use of the motor car. Under the watchful but apparently unenthusiastic eye of his clergy he leaves Bishop's House in his Double Phaeton in 1904.
~ Auckland Diocese

The interior of Sacred Heart Church, Ponsonby, early 1900s.
~ Auckland Diocese

Late nineteenth-century photograph of Saint Mary's Church in Tauranga, with school-age parishioners in the foreground.
~ *A. C. Bellamy*

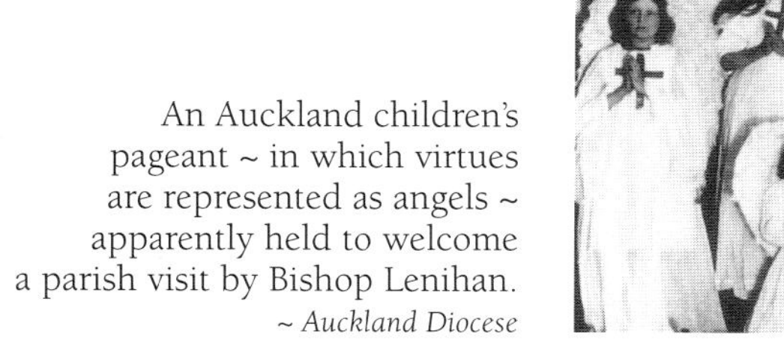
An Auckland children's pageant ~ in which virtues are represented as angels ~ apparently held to welcome a parish visit by Bishop Lenihan.
~ *Auckland Diocese*

calibre of Lenihan's subordinates; and new parishes were created by the progressive subdivision of existing ones when they became too large to be operated as single units.

In 1910 Lenihan's early death (at fifty-two) opened the way for the appointment of the most charismatic and energetic bishop the Church in New Zealand had seen since Patrick Moran. Like Moran, Henry Cleary was Irish — born in County Wexford and trained at Maynooth; like Moran too the new bishop had been an editor of the *Tablet*, from 1898 to 1910. He was already a national figure as a result of this apprenticeship.

As a bishop Cleary would be 'the brightest light of the Church in New Zealand' and 'the intellectual pacemaker of the New Zealand hierarchy'. In addition he was 'a friend of Mark Twain [and] Chesterton and Belloc . . . He exhibited oil paintings and flowers, gave highly successful performances of magic [and] was one of the first passengers on commercial aeroplane flights.'[26] In spite of Cleary s brilliance and versatility — perhaps because of it

Bishop Lenihan presides over what is described as 'opening night in the Pitt Street clubrooms' ~ possibly a celebration of the completion of extensions to Saint Patrick's Cathedral in Auckland. Whatever the occasion it is a men-only affair; and alcohol is being served.
~ *Auckland Diocese*

A glimpse of Bishop Cleary doing what he enjoyed most ~ vigorously discussing religious issues and contemporary events on a marae with Maori parishioners. The Mill Hills on either side of him are Albert Lightheart and Carl Kreijmborg. The marae is in Northland, possibly Pawarenga. Cleary was the first Catholic bishop since Pompallier to speak Maori.
~ Auckland Diocese

— he became an erratic figure and his episcopate seemed often to be on the brink of collapse or scandal.

The issues which Cleary took up with gusto on behalf of the New Zealand Catholic hierarchy included a renewed campaign for state aid to private schools and opposition to the Protestant 'Bible-in-schools' movement (though in this instance Cleary's stand was not supported by all of his fellow bishops). He also learned Maori — the first bishop to do so since Pompallier and Viard — and spent considerable periods touring the backblocks, sometimes by plane, to engage in discussion with his Maori flock. Unlike Redwood and his successor in Wellington, Thomas O'Shea, Bishop Cleary enjoyed the ritual and wordiness of Maori hui. On Auckland's North Shore he established Saint Peter's Catechist Training School for Maori, which later became Hato Petera College.

Within a few years, however, Cleary was causing problems for his episcopal colleagues. One major difficulty was his physical and emotional health. He suffered from 'nervous collapses' which also involved chest and stomach problems. They were possibly a result of overwork and overly intense work and in 1916 the bishop sailed for Europe intending to resign his see. Instead he became a war chaplain in England and France, where he was struck in the

Auckland continued to be the diocese most responsible for innovation. Henry Cleary was the first New Zealand prelate to visit outlying areas ~ especially in Northland ~ by plane. He prepares for take-off in a Walsh brothers flying boat from (appropriately enough) Mission Bay in 1921.
~ Auckland Diocese

Father Francis Bartley, a Marist, was one of fourteen Catholic chaplains who served with the New Zealand armed forces in the First World War. This photograph was taken at a training camp near Nelson in 1916.
~ Marist Archives

helmet by a shell, had his trousers shredded by shrapnel and was twice buried by explosions. All this invigorated him and seemed to restore him to full health. He returned home with all thoughts of resignation forgotten.

Others were not so lucky. The country sent 103,000 men to the war, of whom around 14,000 were Catholic. They were serviced by fourteen chaplains, one for each 1000 soldiers. Several thousand Catholics did not come back (one family, the Caseys of

Father Bartley (in uniform) and Father William Skinner conduct the burial of Brigadier General F. E. Johnston at Bailleul in August 1917. Johnston, an English Catholic officer who served with New Zealand soldiers in France, was remembered by them for 'manly character and robust straightforwardness'. Another New Zealand chaplain, Father James McMenamin, was killed when struck by a shell at Messines two months earlier.
~ *Marist Archives*

Otara in Southland, lost all three sons on a single day in September 1916); many more were injured or gassed. A prominent Catholic lawyer from Stratford, Colonel William George Malone, died on Gallipoli after leading the Wellington Regiment to the top of Chunuk Bair. One of the Army's most popular chaplains, Father James McMenamin, was killed at Messines while conducting a burial. A major effect of the war — on Catholics as on troops from the wider community — was to make the participants more 'New Zealand-centred' than Empire oriented.

After the war, medical problems continued to affect Bishop Cleary's judgment. He opposed Redwood's decision as Metropolitan to campaign against prohibition; he issued a special Auckland catechism which downplayed the Church's condemnation of registry office marriages; he established in 1918 a new publication, the *Month* (later called *Zealandia*), because he had disagreed with many of the opinions of the *Tablet*'s feisty new Irish editor, Father James Kelly (who, among many memorable phrases, referred to Queen Victoria as a 'fat old German woman' and the Minister of Education as a 'monotonous parrot').[27] All of these decisions upset Cleary's fellow bishops. The climax, however, was his treatment of his coadjutor James Liston.

Bishop Henry Cleary's great love of children ~ to whom he was known as Lunky Lee (from Uncle Cleary) ~ is apparent in this photograph of a visit to Karamu. The family are Moroneys; the priest is not identified. Cleary wrote a 'Lunky Lee' column for his paper the *Month* from 1918 until his death in 1929.
~ *Auckland Diocese*

Liston was appointed in 1920 to assist Cleary and to take over from the older man if his health deteriorated further. He was to become New Zealand's longest-serving and most venerated bishop after Redwood. At the beginning of his episcopal career, however, Liston was 'awkward, angular, bookish, stilted in conversation and [unlike his superior] cared little for public acclaim . . .'[28] He was born in Dunedin in 1881 to Irish parents, educated by the Christian Brothers, then sent to the Manly seminary in Sydney at the age of twelve. From there he studied further at Clonliffe College in Dublin and at the Irish College in Rome, where he was ordained. He returned to New Zealand as a Doctor of Divinity and began teaching at Holy Cross College in 1904. He was appointed Rector there in 1910.

When he came to Auckland, Liston had spent twenty-eight out of his thirty-nine years in seminaries. Nobody questioned his piety or his learning; but some, especially an extrovert like Cleary, found that his shyness and austerity made him difficult to deal with. Given those qualities, it was all the more surprising that Liston should be charged with sedition after giving an address at a Saint Patrick's Day concert in the Auckland Town Hall in 1922 — thus becoming the first bishop in the British Empire to be threatened with prosecution for political opinions. Speaking of the Easter 1916 uprising in Dublin he was reported as saying: 'We must not forget the martyrs who died in the fighting in 1916,

The proud and princely Daniel Mannix, Archbishop of Melbourne (wearing buckled shoes) poses outside Bishop's House in Auckland with his fellow Maynooth graduate Henry Cleary, Bishop John McCarthy of Sandhurst, Victoria, and the Auckland coadjutor, James Liston.
~ Auckland Diocese

that glorious Easter . . . I have here a list of 155 men and women who were proud to die for their country. Some were shot. Some were hung and some died on hunger strike, murdered by foreign troops.'[29] The 'foreign troops', of course, were presumed to be British.

All this was said at a time when the Protestant Political Association was at the height of its popularity in New Zealand. Its members believed that to speak in favour of Irish independence — achieved in 1922 — was to support disloyalty to the King and the Empire. When the Mayor of Auckland, James Gunson, claimed that the bishop's speech was 'avowedly and openly disloyal', he was congratulated by members of the PPA and the Orangemen's lodges. Liston, on the other hand, was supported by such prominent Labour Party leaders as Pat Hickey, who was a Catholic of Irish descent, and Tom Bloodworth and John A. Lee, who were not. The case went to trial and the bishop, defended by fiery Wellington lawyer P. J. O'Regan, was acquitted. But the all-Protestant jury added a rider that Liston was 'guilty of a grave indiscretion in using words capable of an interpretation so calculated as to give offence to a large number of the public . . .'[30]

Bishop Cleary, in the United Kingdom when all this occurred, attempted to have the charges dropped through political intervention. At this juncture he fully supported his deputy. After his return to New Zealand and an investigation of actions taken by Liston in his absence, however, he changed his mind. One of the coadjutor's initiatives had been to invite the Knights of the Southern Cross of Australia, a Masonic-like secret society originating in the Knights of Saint Columba in the United Kingdom and the Knights of Columbus in the United States, to establish a branch in Auckland. Cleary abhorred the secrecy of the knights, and the fact that they had the potential to become spies for whatever bishop engaged their loyalty. Although the Auckland or 'Northern State' of the society remained inactive until after Cleary's death, Redwood, who did not share Cleary's scruples on this as on so many other issues, arranged for a 'Southern State' of the knights to be established in Wellington in 1924. Both branches combined to form a national body in 1931. Since 1970 the Knights of the Southern Cross of New Zealand has been a 'confidential' rather than a secret association.[31]

As a result of this and other disagreements with Liston, Bishop Cleary eventually petitioned Rome for the removal of his coadjutor. Among other things, he cited both Liston's Saint Patrick's Day speech and the resulting trial as evidence of his deputy's instability. He went so far as to claim that Liston suffered from hereditary insanity. Bishop Brodie of Christchurch, investigating the charges, concluded that Liston was 'a man of deep spirituality, with an intense love for the Blessed Sacrament . . . a most kindly, thoughtful and generous man . . .' He dismissed any

Bishop Cleary, his health problems at an end at last, lies in state in Saint Patrick's Cathedral in December 1929. His death opened the way for his long-suffering coadjutor, Bishop Liston, to become a figure of authority and respect in his own right.
~ *Auckland Diocese*

This Maori farewell at Howick was part of a huge outpouring of grief that accompanied Bishop Cleary's funeral and burial. He was loved and trusted by his Maori congregation in a way that no bishop had been before or immediately after him.
~ Auckland Diocese

suggestion of insanity and attributed Cleary's accusations to the older man's 'shattered health . . . a nerve-wrecked system'.[32] Bishop Liston retained his post, despite years of 'discouragement and humiliation'; and he succeeded to the see when Cleary died in 1929.

Matthew Brodie, the man chosen to investigate Cleary's accusations against Liston, had been appointed Bishop of Christchurch after Grimes's death in 1915. From an Irish gold-mining family at Coromandel, he was the first New Zealand-born priest to become a Catholic bishop. Brodie had trained at the seminary in Sydney, was parish priest of Waihi in 1912 during the difficult months of the goldminers' strike, and then became parish priest of Parnell and Vicar General of the Auckland Diocese. His appointment to Christchurch was received there with joy and he proved to be a popular, long-serving and hard-working prelate. But, as the first secular bishop in what had been regarded as a Marist diocese, he had lengthy disputes with Marist superiors about the order's tenure of parishes. His relations with individual Marists, however, were at all times courteous and cordial.

To avoid such conflict in Wellington the Vicar General, Thomas O'Shea, who was a Marist, had been appointed coadjutor there in

1913. Like his superior, Archbishop Redwood, O'Shea had narrowly missed out on being a New Zealander. He was born in San Francisco but received all his schooling in New Zealand, being a foundation pupil at Saint Patrick's College and at the Marist seminary at Meeanee. He had been appointed parish priest of Te Aro in Wellington at the early age of thirty-one and was a popular choice as coadjutor. He would need to wait a further twenty-two years, however, to succeed the 'ageing' Francis Redwood.

In Dunedin, Bishop Verdon succumbed to the 1918 influenza epidemic and was followed in 1920 by another Irishman, James Whyte. Born in Kilkenny in 1868 and Chancellor of the Sydney Archdiocese at the time of his Dunedin appointment, Whyte was viewed as a 'conservative and cautious man, rather autocratic in his style, a churchman of the old school. He possessed considerable intellectual ability and a deep faith and the administration of the smallest and slowest-growing of the New Zealand dioceses was no great task for a man of his capacity. Yet in his twenty years of active work as a bishop he does not seem to have exerted much positive leadership either in his own diocese or in New Zealand at large. Rather he seems to have been almost a symbol of the rule of a dead law which was to spread its paralysing influence over the life of the Church in the next couple of decades . . .'[33]

Bishop Matthew Brodie (right) is exposed to the full force of a Chatham Islands gale at Owenga in the course of a visit to the islands in 1929. The priest at left is Father John McMonagle. Eleven of this group, mostly Maori, had just been confirmed.
~ *V. McSweeney*

Four of the country's longest-serving bishops gathered at Mosgiel in 1932 for the opening of a new wing at Holy Cross College. From left ~ Matthew Brodie (Bishop of Christchurch 1915–1943), Francis Redwood (Wellington 1874–1935), James Whyte (Dunedin 1920–1957) and James Liston (Auckland 1929-1970).
~ *Auckland Diocese*

Opposite ~ The years between the First and Second World Wars brought a significant increase in the number of churches built in the two northern dioceses. Many more were now being constructed of more permanent material than wood. This brick church, dedicated to the Sacred Heart, is being blessed and opened by Archbishop Francis Redwood at Havelock South in December 1924.
~ *Marist Archives*

This 'paralysing influence' may have been in part a consequence of a period of unprecedented episcopal stability. Of those appointed as bishops or coadjutors by 1920, James Liston would remain in office in Auckland until 1970, Thomas O'Shea in Wellington until 1954, James Whyte in Dunedin until 1947 and Matthew Brodie in Christchurch until 1943. All of these men were Irish or of Irish descent — as were the next batch of coadjutors (Hugh O'Neill and John Kavanagh in Dunedin from 1943 and 1949 respectively, and Peter McKeefrey in Wellington from 1947).

According to Ernest Simmons, 'the twenties really set the style for the Church for the next generation. The primary emphasis was on providing churches, priests and schools; to continue contact with the Church through the Holy Name Society [which

Irish parish priest, Dean James Joseph Hackett, pictured here with his parish committee at Paeroa in the early 1920s. He had arrived in New Zealand in 1885 and served also in Dargaville, Saint Patrick's Cathedral in Auckland and Ellerslie. The woman seated two away from the left of the dean is his sister, who emigrated from Ireland to join him as his housekeeper and give him at least one link with the family he had left behind. It was not usual at this time for Irish priests to make return visits home.

~ Leone Shaw

Bishop Matthew Brodie hosts visiting Archbishop of Melbourne Daniel Mannix at a meeting of the Greymouth Hibernians in 1924. Mannix, Irish-born and educated and seen as the leader of Irish Catholicism in Australia, had expressed a wish to meet New Zealand Irish. The Greymouth Hibernians had been the first branch of the famous Irish 'lodge' to be established in New Zealand. The organisation was a Catholic benefit society which, in return for premiums, paid out benefits for members' illnesses, hospital treatment and funeral expenses. The Hibernians also had a strong social and cultural function and helped Catholic men retain contact with their predominantly Irish roots.
~ Patrick O'Farrell

Opposite
The Children of Mary, which encouraged Catholic girls to be prayerful, ladylike and chaste and to model their lives on the Mother of Christ, was the most popular sodality in New Zealand parishes in the years prior to the Second World War. These Children of Mary from the Auckland Diocese take part in a Eucharistic procession at Sacred Heart College, Ponsonby, in 1932.
~ Auckland Diocese

For Catholic boys the equivalent of membership of the Children of Mary was the training and spiritual guidance they received for their role as altar boys (girls were not permitted to serve in the sanctuary for Mass and Benediction of the Blessed Sacrament). In this group Fathers O'Flynn and Curran pose with their altar boys in Auckland.
~ Auckland Diocese

was established in New Zealand in 1926 and became the only truly national Catholic organisation], the Children of Mary and a variety of women's societies; to develop greater participation in the Mass by encouraging the use of the missal. The Catholic community was turned inwards on itself, looking to its own affairs, not participating very much in the general work of the community at large. Its attitude towards the outsider was defensive and triumphalistic, and the Catholic journals of the period tend to rely heavily on a rather smug apologetic and cosy praise of "our" churches, "our" bishops and "our" schools. An attempt to set up a chair of theology in the Otago University on an ecumenical basis met with a resolute refusal to participate from the Catholic

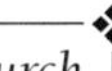

Catholic organisations, like the Maritime Club in Wellington, organised dances for young men and women. Guests here include Archbishop O'Shea and the club chaplain, Father J. Fletcher.
~ Marist Archives

Opposite ~ A procession of the Blessed Sacrament in Wellington in February 1940 in the grounds of Sacred Heart Convent, Island Bay, part of the New Zealand Eucharistic Congress. Such processions were subsequently held annually at Sacred Heart on the feast of Christ the King, observed on the last Sunday in October.
~ Marist Archives

bishops. Catholics were even refused the sacraments if they sent their children to state schools. Even participation in the Boy Scouts and Girl Guides was discouraged . . . It was as though the establishing of a Catholic school system as a rival to the state system was somehow influencing all Catholic life, so that any kind of participation in secular organisations was being seen as immoral.'[34]

One symptom of the triumphalism of these inter-war years was the series of Eucharistic Congresses held throughout the Catholic world. These were highly organised events in which Catholics processed through city streets and attended Mass and Eucharistic adoration in spacious public places, such as parks or sports stadiums. The 1940 Congress in Wellington coincided with the New Zealand Centennial, commemorating the signing of the Treaty of Waitangi and the induction of the country into the British Empire in 1840. New Zealand delegations also attended Congresses in Sydney in 1928 and Dublin in 1932.

High Mass celebrated in the chapel at Holy Cross College, Mosgiel, during the Second World War. The rate of New Zealand priestly vocations remained high through the 1940s and 1950s but declined sharply from the late 1960s.
~ *Holy Cross College*

Opposite ~ These first communicants were photographed at Saint Bernadette's parish, Dunedin, in 1942. They include Glenys Cusack (top left), who was to be the mother of the Labour Member of Parliament Lianne Dalziel, and (in front of her) Brian Macdonnell, who would become Labour MP for Dunedin Central.
~ *Glenys Dalziel*

A nuptial Mass at Saint Mary's Church in Meeanee in the 1930s. Such Masses were celebrated only when Catholic married Catholic. 'Mixed marriages' were performed outside the sanctuary and without Mass.
~ *Marist Archives*

Eileen Duggan (1894–1972), unofficial Catholic poet laureate. Her poems and historical articles were published in the Catholic and secular press for over fifty years. She was especially well known to readers of the *Catholic School Journal*, which went into every convent school. Her parents were Irish (born in County Kerry). Eileen grew up in Marlborough. While she had a short career as a teacher, the greater part of her adult life was spent living quietly with a sister in Wellington. She was one of the first writers in New Zealand to be awarded a 'literary pension'.
~ *Pat Lawlor Collection*

The experience of growing up in these years of Catholic self-containment was well evoked by Catholic writers. Eileen Duggan, for example, a woman of fragile health, born on the Wairau Plain of Irish parentage, celebrated the verities and the certitudes of her Faith. Her poems, published widely in the *Tablet* and the *Catholic School Journal*, are infused with a sense of Irish and New Zealand history, and with the apprehension of God in nature:

> Who loves to sit and dream God in the sun,
> Who hears His voice at dawn among the birds,
> And knows His joy is with the yellow bees
> Adrowse with honey in laburnum trees![35]

And:

> On a Marlborough foreland there is a bay
> Facing the east, where the auroral ray
> Falls level with the great Pacific flow

Opposite ~ The Basilica of the Sacred Heart in Wellington, designed by Francis Petre to replace Bishop Viard's Saint Mary's Cathedral, destroyed by fire in 1898, was one of the few New Zealand churches built in baroque style. Here the altar is decorated for the 'Forty Hours' exposition of the Blessed Sacrament ~ a devotion that was especially popular in New Zealand Catholic churches in the inter-war years.
~ *Marist Archives*

That stretches landless, boundless to the Horn;
Upon the foreland, wild with bine and thorn,
There is a well; and older folk who know
Call it Pezant's, bidding their children pray
For him who on his journey to the Sounds
Cooled his parched mouth and washed the little wounds
Made by rocks and boughs that pierce and flay.[36]

Duggan also wrote copious historical articles for the Catholic press, especially for the *Month* and the *Tablet*; under the *nom de plume* 'Pippa', she produced a weekly women's page for the *Tablet* for more than four decades. This range of published imaginative and non-fiction material ensured that she was the most influential New Zealand Catholic writer of her time.

Dan Davin grew up between the wars in Irish-Catholic Southland — 'not so much a community as a tribe . . . bound together by their fierce loyalty, rigid faith and common struggle against adversity . . . [But] these people also shared their wit and laughter, their love of story-telling from a common storehouse of legend and myth, and an unselfconscious pleasure in song and conversation.'[37] Davin's recreation of his childhood within this tribe is vivid and resonant:

'He had a revelation. In a flash, like what happened to Saint Paul, only not frightening. Green was the colour of God. It was the colour of the grass and of the trees and of the sea and of all the best things, of God's things. Green was the colour of Ireland. In Ireland, his father said, everything was green. Even the fairies. Green was Ireland's National Colour. And the Irish were the best people. Even here in New Zealand you knew that. And all the Irish were Catholics. Their colour was green. God's colour was green. That proved it. The Irish were God's green people. So their green God was the real God . . . Now he was wonderfully glad . . . He would have liked to have somebody to tell about it . . . God was green and Irish and a Catholic.'[38]

And the experience that all Catholic convent-school children remembered:

'Most of the kids were Protestants. They'd very likely go to Hell when they died for singing:

Catholic dogs
Jump like frogs,
Don't eat meat on Friday.

Then, when Mick and his friends sang:

Protestant dogs
Jump like frogs,
Do eat meat on Friday

both sides would pick up stones out of the gravelly road and

Maurice Duggan (1922–74) was another writer born in New Zealand of Irish parents. He was educated by Marist Brothers in Auckland and a brother of his became a priest. Duggan's practice of his faith lapsed in adulthood but he continued to write vivid stories inspired by his Catholic upbringing. Frank Sargeson, doyen of New Zealand letters, considered Duggan the most promising of his protégés.
~ *Barbara Duggan*

begin to fight. But, of course, that was only in the evening on the way home from school.'[39]

Maurice Duggan, no relation to Eileen and rather less reconciled to his culture of origin, wrote of 'the sad Irish bravura; the drear Irish Catholicism; the Irish syndrome — booze, melancholy and guilt; the pointless loud pride — for what had they to be proud of, each man a Joseph in his coat of bright verbs?' But even describing the apostasy of an altar boy Duggan recalls the splendour as well as the dross:

'The ritual, that was the first thing you thought of. The fine patterns on the vestments, the gold chalice, the glinting, false

A Catholic writers' conference in Wellington in the late 1940s. Notable authors there included Eileen Duggan and the romantic novelist Nelle Scanlan (front row, third and fourth from left). The organiser was the Wellington journalist and State Literary Fund secretary Pat Lawlor (standing, second left). The conference made little impact on New Zealand writing because of its insistence on overtly applying religious and moral issues to professional considerations.
~ Pat Lawlor Collection

stones in the bookstand, the elaborate and intricate reredos, the tallshining candlesticks. And the dimness, the faint omniscient yesterday smell, the nighttime odour of stale incense, the broken light through the church windows . . . But the biggest thing was the latin. Strange. A dead language, unchanging, passing without inflection or life . . . the latin seemed always to roll over the seats and the people, back into the walls and the bell tower . . . In nomine Patris, et Filii, et Spiritus Sancti, Amen. Ite missa est. The first words and the last. Go, the Mass is ended . . . Praying and the procession of priest and altar boys back into the sacristy. In there you bow before the brass-polished crucifix and then shrug off the feeling of tension you have had all the time.'[40]

Ruth Park, educated during the Depression in Te Kuiti and Auckland by Mary MacKillop's Sisters of Saint Joseph of the Sacred

Heart, 'loved' most of the nuns who taught her. '[Three] or four have been models for me throughout life. Sisters Serenus, Hilarion, Laurencia, and above all Bertille . . . Their brown shadows are always with me, so that I close doors gently, sit with my feet together, tend to be formal rather than otherwise, and believe that meanness and discourtesy are the mark of the ill-bred. I also remember that a spoonful of honey catches more flies than a pint of vinegar, and that life gives back to us what we give to it.'[41] Park too was a prolific contributor to the *Catholic School Journal*.

O glorious Saint Michael, Prince of the heavenly host and Protector of the Universal Church, defend us against all our enemies visible and invisible, and permit us not to fall under their cruel tyranny; preserve us also from all spiritual and temporal dangers, particularly from fire and contagious diseases. Amen

Much of the sectarian rivalry of those days was fought out on the rugby field. Rugby, a national sport in which Catholic boys could excel by dint of hard training and determination, assumed a large role in the culture of existing colleges and new ones (Saint Bede's in Christchurch opened in 1911, Saint Kevin's in Oamaru in 1927, Saint Pat's Silverstream, 1931). And Catholics who made the All Blacks, such as the Brownlie brothers and the Blake brothers, were heroes to their coreligionists.

Debating too was an activity in which Catholic schools excelled, the girls colleges — Teschemaker's near Oamaru, the Sacred Heart convents at Island Bay, Wellington, and Remuera, Auckland, known subsequently as Erskine College and Baradene — doing as well as the boys. In the male colleges, one of the goals of teaching debating skills was to lift the percentage of Catholic men in the professions, where they were long assumed to be held back by Protestant prejudice, masonic conspiracy or Anglican old-boy networks. Catholics in general applauded as their second- and third-generation-Irish brethren broke into first the ranks of the law (men such as J. B. Gallan and Humphrey O'Leary who became Supreme Court judges in 1935 and 1946), and then medicine (eminent doctors such as physician and cardiologist Charles Burns, who was also widely involved in community organisations).

Catholic women at this time — like New Zealand women in general — were not expected to seek careers. The goals set for them were likely to be those of Little Irish Mother or nun. The Catholic Women's League, which was established in the Auckland Diocese by Bishop Liston in 1931 with a motto of 'Faith and Service', largely upheld and celebrated the role of women as homemakers. With later branches opened in Christchurch (1936), Wellington (1944) and Dunedin (1949), the league became a national organisation in 1949. It would be responsible for much valuable parish and community work over the next five decades and allowed a national Catholic voice to be heard on issues such as contraception and abortion.

A more radical women's organisation, the Grail, was established in all dioceses in the late 1930s. It had the particular

Members of the Catholic feminist organisation the Grail march in Wellington in 1938 to mark the centenary of the arrival in New Zealand of Bishop Pompallier. This procession of local Catholic groups, one of dozens of celebratory events throughout the country, walked the length of Cambridge Terrace from the Basin Reserve to Saint Patrick's College.
~ Julia Moriarty

encouragement of Bishop Brodie in Christchurch. 'This international movement . . . began in Holland in 1921 to unite married and single women of varying backgrounds in a common effort to bring spiritual values to modern society . . . [It] was a far-sighted attempt to channel into the service of Christ and his church the enthusiasms of the Feminist movement . . .'[42] The impetus of the Grail in New Zealand was lost, however, as a result of Brodie's death in 1943 and the intervention of other social priorities after the outbreak of the Second World War.

Some Catholic women achieved high professional status, especially in teaching, nursing or charitable work. And many such achievers were also nuns. The Mater Misericordiae Hospital in Auckland, for example, was staffed by Sisters of Mercy; the Lewisham Hospitals in Christchurch and Wellington by the Little Company of Mary.

Suzanne Aubert, now known as Mother Mary Joseph Aubert, had brought her Sisters of Compassion to Wellington in 1899

Sisters Baptista and de Sales with their first 'begging pram', which they pushed through the commercial centre of Wellington in the early 1900s seeking donations of food for the Home of Compassion in Buckle Street. Their Daughters of Our Lady of Compassion habits, designed by Suzanne Aubert, were in the style of nineteenth-century French religious dress.
~ Sisters of Compassion Archive

and established a soup kitchen, day-care nursery, home for incurables and — in 1907 — Our Lady's Home of Compassion in Island Bay. She became a national figure for her work with foundlings, the ill and the disabled. She opened another home in Auckland in 1910. The hierarchy, however, were not wholly approving of Aubert's work or her personality and she had fights with Bishops Cleary, O'Shea and Redwood reminiscent of her

A corner of the 'Foundlings Ward' at Mother Aubert's new Home of Compassion in Island Bay, opened in 1905.
~ Sisters of Compassion Archive

battles half a century earlier with Pompallier and Croke. Redwood, for example, wanted her to restrict her efforts to Catholics, which she refused to do. In 1913, at the age of seventy-six, Mother Aubert did what Mother Mary MacKillop of Australia had had to do forty years earlier. She went to Rome to seek papal recognition of her order, which would free her from the jurisdiction of local bishops. The war in Europe stranded her and she was unable to return to Wellington until 1920; but she had the decree she sought. Her Sisters of Compassion survived her with homes in Auckland, Wellington, Wanganui, Silverstream, Timaru and Carterton; in Australia in Broken Hill and Wagga Wagga; and in Fiji and Tonga.

Mother Aubert's vision and example — her insistence on seeing Christ in every person who needed help, her refusal while doing so to distinguish between Catholic and non-Catholic, Maori and Pakeha — were among the most pervasive and enduring forces to emerge from the Catholic Church in New Zealand.[43]

Father Francis Vernon Douglas, originally from Johnsonville, Wellington who, after training at Mosgiel, joined the Columban missionary order and was posted to Pililla in the Philippines. In July 1943 he was taken into custody by the Japanese occupation forces and was never heard from again. He is believed to have been tortured and killed because of his refusal to reveal to the Japanese authorities what Philippino guerillas had said to him under the seal of the confessional.
~ Holy Cross College

Other orders too became involved in foreign missions, particularly in the Pacific Islands. Marist fathers, brothers and sisters worked in Tonga, Samoa, Fiji and the Solomons. Father Emmet McHardy became especially well known: after his premature death in 1933 from tubercular meningitis a selection of his letters home entitled *Blazing the Trail* was a best seller among New Zealand Catholics. Some New Zealanders joined orders such as the Columbans which specialised in missions to other Third World countries. One of them, Father Francis Vernon Douglas, was killed by Japanese occupation forces in the Philippines in 1943 in circumstances that may have amounted to martyrdom (he was apparently tortured for refusing to reveal information passed to him in the confessional by partisan fighters).[44]

Sisters Blaise and Dominica of the Sisters of Our Lady of the Missions spent the summer of 1929–30 conducting a catechism school on the Chatham Islands. Plans to establish a convent school run by this religious order at Waitangi collapsed, but Missionary Sisters of the Society of Mary staffed the Chathams cottage hospital from 1945.
~ *V. McSweeney*

Suzanne Aubert and Francis Redwood were among the last living links with the Church's missionary era in New Zealand. Aubert died in October 1926, aged ninety-one, widely regarded in the quieter final years of her life as a saint. Francis Redwood followed her in January 1935 after a record six decades as a bishop. The year of his death was also a watershed in New Zealand politics. The first Labour Government came to office with a Catholic Prime

Catholic womanhood at prayer. This phalanx of laity and nuns (mostly Sisters of Mercy with Sisters of Saint Joseph of Cluny in the centre) turned out for Father Peyton's rosary crusade in Christchurch in 1954. A little over a decade later most orders of nuns had shed restrictive features of their habits, such as starched wimples. Not present on this occasion were the Carmelites, an enclosed order in Christchurch since 1933. They would be the group least changed by the Vatican II reforms.
~ *Christchurch Diocese*

Minister (New Zealand's third), Michael Joseph Savage, and a cabinet that contained others of the Faith (Dan Sullivan, Paddy Webb, Tim Armstrong).

The attitude of the Catholic hierarchy to the Labour Movement had always been ambivalent. Many of Labour's leaders had been radical socialists, dedicated in their early days to smashing the existing social and industrial order. On the other hand, many of them also had Irish-Catholic backgrounds; and after the years of the Great Depression it was likely that a majority of Catholics, especially those living in the poorer sections of society, supported Labour. After 1935 Savage's portrait was commonly hung in Catholic homes alongside those of the Sacred Heart and the Blessed Virgin. Meanwhile the Prime Minister mended fences with his Church. Savage established a close relationship with James Liston and returned to the practice of his Faith during a long bout with terminal cancer. He was buried from a Catholic Church in 1940.

The body of Michael Joseph Savage, first Labour Prime Minister, is carried from the Auckland Railway Station *en route* for Saint Patrick's Cathedral in March 1940. Savage resumed the practice of his faith while suffering from cancer in the last months of his life.
~ Auckland Diocese

The new Prime Minister, Peter Fraser, and his deputy, Walter Nash, were not Catholic — but they assiduously cultivated Catholic leaders and voters, and Fraser was an especially close confidant of Archbishop O'Shea.

It was Labour that led the country into what was for many people the second world war in their lifetime. Again Catholics played their full part as soldiers, sailors, airmen, home guardsmen and chaplains; again there were casualties abroad and hardships at home. This time, however, New Zealand was invaded: not by enemy forces but by those of an ally. Tens of thousands of American servicemen trained and recreated around Auckland and Wellington. A high proportion were Catholic and swelled congregations and collection plates in parishes close to their bases. They gave New Zealand Catholics wider experience of other Catholics who had not grown up in a predominantly Irish-derived Church — as did Catholics who came to New Zealand as refugees from Hitler's Europe, such as Lisl Heller from Austria and Maria Dronke from Germany. The latter, an actor and voice teacher who died in 1987, was remembered as 'volatile, brimful of temperament and never tepid'.[45]

Polish children in a special camp created for them at Pahiatua in November 1944. Over 700 of these children, who had been orphaned or separated from their families by the war in Europe, were granted asylum in New Zealand through the Polish Red Cross. Most were Catholic, and most remained in New Zealand after the war and introduced another strain of European Catholicism to the history of the Church in New Zealand.
~ *National Archives*

At least one initiative taken during the war had major consequences in the years of peace that followed. In 1941 Father Frank Bennett of Dunedin organised a study week at Holy Cross College that attracted forty priests from all over the country. He introduced them to the concept of the 'lay apostolate' and to a programme for involving youth in the work of the Church originally developed in Europe by a Belgian priest, Joseph Cardijn. This called for the setting up of groups to study the Gospels and then analyse contemporary society to see how it measured up to Gospel standards. Where it did not, the groups would work to transform it according to Christian principles. The watchwords were, 'See, judge, act.'[46]

From this meeting the Catholic Youth Movement spread

Another Catholic minority in New Zealand was the Italian community, largely engaged in fishing in Cook Strait. Italians had been migrating to New Zealand since the late nineteenth century, particularly from the Aeolian island of Stromboli, and brought with them many of the customs of their culture. Here Archbishop McKeefrey and parish priest Father Jack Reader row out to perform the annual blessing of the fishing fleet at Island Bay in the 1950s. The sculler is fisherman Frank Della Barca.
~ *Dominion*

through all four dioceses and was to be promoted strongly in Auckland by Dr Reginald Delargy, in Wellington by Father David O'Neill, in Christchurch by Father John Curnow and in Dunedin by Father Bennett. All these priests generated considerable commitment to the principle of 'Catholic Action'. 'For the first time young Catholics were asked to . . . undertake positive action in their offices, factories and homes to make New Zealand society more Christian.'[47] Among the laity who participated and made their mark subsequently working for a variety of social and professional causes were Patricia Burns, Tom Williams, Des Nolan, Ray Scott, Maurice McIntyre, Des Hurley, Robert Consedine and Jim Anderton. Williams, after a period working as an accountant, would eventually become Cardinal Archbishop of Wellington; Anderton would go on to make a career in politics, first in the Labour Party and then as leader of NewLabour and the Alliance. Offshoots of the CYM included the League of Christian Families

Father Frank Bennett was a popular lecturer at Holy Cross Seminary. In 1941 he organised a national seminar that introduced 'Catholic Action' and the Catholic Youth Movement to New Zealand. These initiatives were to engage two generations of idealistic young Catholics.
~ Holy Cross College

Diocesan youth leaders meet with Father John Curnow, CYM director, at Rosary House in Christchurch in 1952. Curnow was a charismatic priest who built a strong rapport with those among whom he worked. He also took a leading role in the reformation of Church attitudes and practices that occurred after the Second Vatican Council.
~ Mary Stuart

By the 1950s the Mercy Sisters had taught and nursed in New Zealand for more than a hundred years. This classroom scene is at Saint Mary's College in Christchurch.
~ Patrick O'Farrell

From the 1940s to the 1960s Catholic girls who had just left school 'came out' at annual Charity Balls and were presented to their bishop. The organisation was generally undertaken by branches of the Catholic Women's League. This one was for former pupils of Sacred Heart Convent in Hamilton and their partners. Their former teachers, Sisters of Our Lady of the Missions, watch from the sideline.
~ Kath Haliday

Basketball ~ later called netball ~ was almost as important a sport at Catholic girls schools as rugby was at boys colleges. This team from Saint Anthony's Convent in Wanganui won the regional competition shield in 1953.
~ E. P. O'Leary

(established in Auckland by Alfred Bennett) and the Christian Family Movement, which was at its strongest in the late 1950s.[48]

By war's end the highly revered Bishop Matthew Brodie of Christchurch had died and been replaced briefly (1944–50) by the Irish-Australian Patrick Lyons. After nearly three decades' experience of Brodie's warmth and charm, the diocese found Bishop Lyons a coldly formal man; he was not popular with either his priests or his laity.[49] In 1950, however, he was appointed auxiliary to Cardinal Gilroy in Sydney. His successor in Christchurch was Edward Joyce, a former local parish priest and army chaplain. Joyce's popularity never matched Brodie's but he did preside over a fourteen-year period of unprecedented growth in the diocese. His final years, however, were blighted by illness. In Dunedin the ailing Bishop Whyte continued to direct the affairs of his diocese from his sickbed and wore out his first coadjutor, Hugh O'Neill, who resigned in 1949. Meanwhile Archbishop O'Shea, now showing the effects of senility, had been given a coadjutor in Wellington in 1947: Peter McKeefrey, who had been editor of *Zealandia* for twenty years and secretary to Bishop Liston.

These changes left James Liston as the senior and dominant figure in the New Zealand Catholic hierarchy by the 1950s. In

Above & opposite ~ Saint Patrick's Day parties remained a popular way to celebrate Irish ethnicity and Catholicism in the years following the Second World War. In these pictures taken in Wanganui on Saint Patrick's night 1962, Terry Mullins raises an Irish tune on the fiddle and Dinnie Donovan sings, watched by Brian Mullins, Helen O'Neill and Tim O'Leary.
~ E. P. O'Leary

Opposite ~ In the immediate post-war years Irish dancing was still a popular activity at Catholic girls schools, and a feature of Saint Patrick's Day celebrations and competitions. These girls, surnames Kyne, Shanahan, O'Regan and Horgan, won prizes in a national competition in 1949.
~ Marist Archives

recognition of his status and his widely recognised piety he was made an Assistant at the Papal Throne in 1950 and Archbishop in 1953. The following year he celebrated the fiftieth anniversary of his ordination. He was not, of course, Metropolitan of New Zealand. But Archbishop McKeefrey, who assumed this position on O'Shea's death in 1954, was Liston's protégé and hence for some years at least operated in the shadow of his mentor. So long as the bishops were in agreement about what was good for the Church in New Zealand there were no serious problems. But as the 1950s merged into the 1960s and more radical changes to the Church's policies and structures were proposed, Liston's growing conservatism and 'creeping infallibility' imposed stress on his colleagues and the priests in his diocese.[50]

In 1957 Bishop Whyte's death allowed his able coadjutor John Kavanagh to succeed to the see of Dunedin. The following year Dr Reginald Delargy, an enthusiastic reformist, became James Liston's uncomfortable coadjutor in Auckland. By now major difficulties were in sight for the Church in New Zealand. Although religious congregations continued to establish themselves in New Zealand (the Cenacle Sisters from the United States in 1953, for example; and Cistercians from Ireland, who opened the Southern

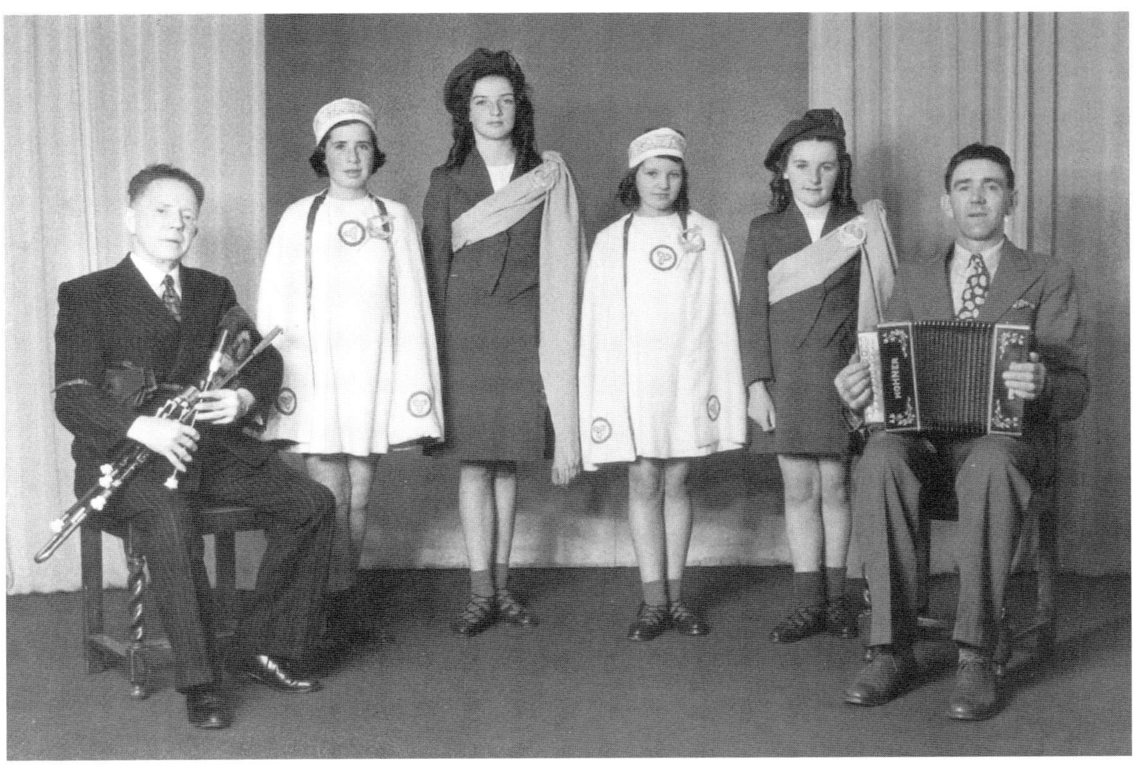

New Zealand and Irish Catholics, particularly those old enough to remember 'the Troubles' of the early 1920s, retained an interest in Irish politics. They revered Eamon de Valera, surviving head of the 1916 rebellion, who was Prime Minister of Eire from 1932 to 1959, and president until 1973. When 'Dev' visited Wellington in 1948 Irish clergy and laity turned out to see him, hear him and ask for his autograph. The priests with him in this photograph are Fathers Pat Timoney and Dan Healy.
~ Pat Lawlor Collection

Star Monastery at Kopu in Hawke's Bay in 1954), they were not teaching orders. And numbers of Catholic children were growing at a faster rate than the recruitment of religious teachers; and about half these teachers were still drawn from abroad, especially from Ireland — a country whose Church did not attempt to maintain an alternative system of education as New Zealand did. A national campaign and petition for State aid to Catholic schools organised by the Holy Name Society in 1956 ('Hear the case') had produced no initiatives in that direction from either of the major parties in the New Zealand Parliament. In the course of the campaign, a modest degree of sectarianism was stirred up by Archbishop McKeefrey's statement that, in the event of future wars, he might counsel Catholic men not to enlist for the armed forces unless New Zealand governments supported the Catholic education system.

Other major changes in New Zealand demography had implications for the Church. Maori, who until the 1950s had lived almost entirely in small rural communities, were now moving into the towns and cities in increasing numbers. Most local authorities were unprepared for this migration. Affordable housing was unavailable, there were virtually no facilities for Maori to practise their culture in the cities, and the Church, with the possible exception of the Christchurch Diocese, had made little provision for Maori pastorates in urban areas.

One who made the move to the city at this time was Whina Cooper of Te Rarawa. She brought her family from the Hokianga to Auckland in the early 1950s. In 1951 she was elected foundation president of the Maori Women's Welfare League, the first national Maori organisation, and she used the mana of this position to try to persuade Archbishop Liston and the Mill Hills to do more for Catholic Maori in Auckland. Neither the archbishop nor the priests concerned reacted well to being berated by a woman — and by this woman in particular (who complained that the Church was still treating Maori like 'errant children'). They were slow to respond. Cooper eventually set up an Auckland Maori Catholic Society, which raised sufficient money to build a Catholic urban marae, Te Unga Waka at Epsom, in the mid-1960s. She had the satisfaction of seeing her nephew, Father Henare Tate of Motuti, ordained as the second Maori Catholic priest. She herself attracted

Father Wiremu Te Awhitu, first Maori ordained by the Catholic Church, is greeted by pupils of Saint Joseph's Convent School, Panguru, in 1944.
~ *Whina Cooper*

Dame Whina Cooper, known as Whaea o te Motu (Mother of the Nation), was the most prominent lay member of the New Zealand Catholic Church in the last decades of her life. Here she addresses a meeting at Panguru, Hokianga, in 1983.
~ Michael King

Overleaf (p.176) ~ Mass at Saint Mary of the Angels, Wellington, in the 1950s. A decade later the altar would be brought forward, the celebrating priest would face the congregation, and English would be the language of worship in place of Latin.
~ Marist Archives

a reputation for both sanctity (Auckland lawyer Kevin Ryan called her 'a New Zealander in the tradition of Mother Teresa of Calcutta') and belligerency. By the time she died in 1994 Whina Cooper was a Dame, a member of the Order of New Zealand, and widely known as Te Whaea o te Motu — the 'Mother of the Nation'.[51]

Meanwhile changes in ecclesiastical direction were initiated from a wholly unexpected quarter. In 1958 the frail and ascetic Pope Pius XII died after a nineteen-year pontificate. He was succeeded by Angelo Roncalli, Patriarch of Venice, a seventy-seven-year-old pastoral figure from a Bergamese peasant family. He took the name of John XXIII and was expected to be an interim pope. Less than five years later he was dead. But in those five years he had set in motion a policy of 'aggiornamento' — a throwing open of the windows of the Catholic Church to expose the musty institution to fresh air.

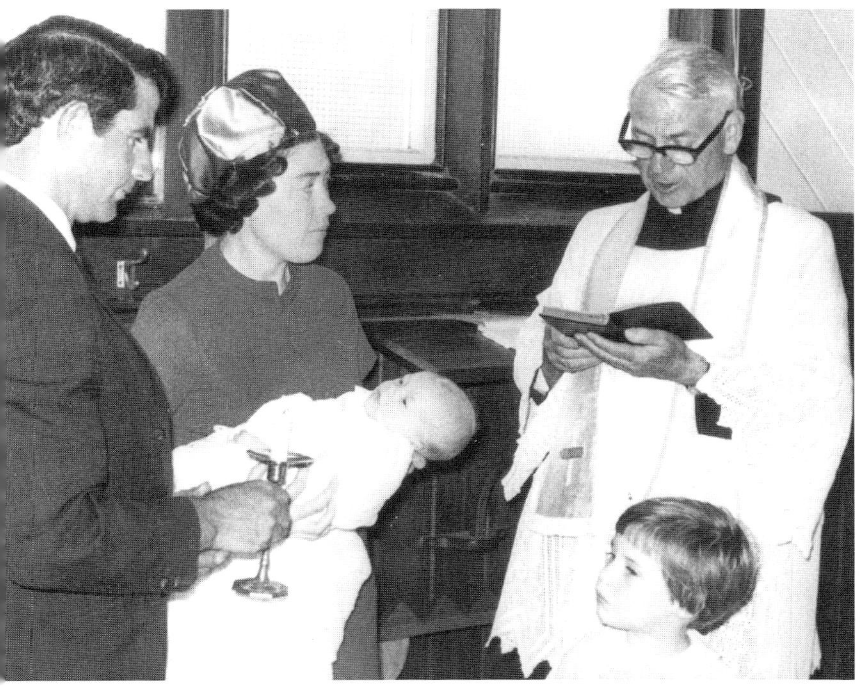

The Vatican Council's encouragement of individual Catholics to take responsibility for their own moral decisions and spiritual welfare had unexpected results. One was the appearance of public demonstrations against the decisions of bishops in Auckland and Christchurch. In this instance (above) Christchurch Catholics protest against a decision of Bishop Brian Ashby to sell the diocese's Maryknoll property, which was to be turned into a carpark. Most Catholics continued to practise their faith in traditional ways, however. Here (left) Tyrone O'Leary of Wanganui is baptised in Saint Mary's Church by Father Lawrence Smith in 1970.
~ Robert Consedine & E. P. O'Leary

HOLY NAME SOCIETY

The bishops who would lead New Zealand Catholics through the reforms of the Vatican Council era (from left) ~ Owen Sneddon (auxiliary Wellington, 1962–81); Reginald Delargy (auxiliary Auckland, 1958–70; Bishop of Auckland 1970–74; Archbishop of Wellington, 1974–79); John Kavanagh (Dunedin, 1957–85); James Liston (Auckland, 1929–70); Brian Ashby (Christchurch, 1964–85); and Peter McKeefrey (Wellington, 1954–73). Of these, only Archbishop Liston ~ because of his age ~ did not attend sessions of the Vatican Council.
~ Auckland Diocese

The major fruit of Roncalli's papacy was his summoning of the Second Vatican Council, which he called upon to 'restore the simple and pure lines which the face of Jesus' Church wore at its birth'. The council met for the first time in October 1962 and continued for another four years. Its decisions and reverberations were wide-ranging. In New Zealand they would bring about a transformation of the Catholic Church and its members on a scale never before seen in its 125-year history.

❖

EPILOGUE

Since Vatican II ~ A New Zealand Identity

THE SECOND VATICAN COUNCIL met in four convocations of bishops in Rome between October 1962 and December 1965. Its major measures of reform were announced in the Documents on the Liturgy (1963), the Church (1964), Ecumenism (1964) and Religious Life (1965). Other key statements came in the Declaration on Religious Freedom and the Pastoral Constitution on the Church in the Modern World (1965). The religious and secular media speedily communicated these proposals to Catholics around the world. This process set up an expectation of and a momentum for change that took everybody — bishops included — by surprise.

All the New Zealand Catholic bishops, apart from James Liston, attended at least one of the convocations (Archbishop Liston's age — eighty-one the year the council began — was a restricting factor; but it was also true that of all the New Zealand hierarchy he was least in sympathy with the changes proposed). Those who were initially most enthusiastic about the introduction of post-

Opposite ~ In November 1986 Pope John Paul II came to New Zealand, the first reigning Pontiff to make such a journey (though in 1973, as Cardinal Karol Wojtyla, he had visited Polish compatriots in Auckland and Wellington). Here — wearing a Maori cloak and greenstone pectoral cross — he greets New Zealand Catholics at a reception and open-air Mass in the Auckland Domain. His Holiness is flanked by Doris Vercoe and Dan Whata. In subsequent days he visited Wellington and Christchurch.
~ *NZ Herald*

Council reforms were Reginald Delargy (Liston's assistant until 1970 and then Bishop of Auckland in his own right) and Owen Sneddon, auxiliary bishop of Wellington from 1962.

Seminarians at Holy Cross college in 1966 were inspired by the spectacle of Bishop Delargy standing before them, brandishing a bound volume of Council documents and declaring: 'This is our gospel. This is what marks the path for the future. It will be up to you people to work out the details.' By that time it was clear that an era of unprecedented ecclesiastical reform was under way. That same class of seminarians had required Latin as a prerequisite for their studies; after ordination, however, they would never be called upon to celebrate a full Latin Mass.

By 1970 the Mass was said in New Zealand entirely in English or Maori. Altars were moved towards church congregations and priests faced their people as they conducted the new liturgy. Prayers and hymns judged to be archaic or unduly sentimental were discarded; new ones were composed that included reference to New Zealand seasons and metaphors. The sacrament of Confession would now be offered — for those who wanted it — on a face to face basis and called Reconciliation. Emphasis would be placed increasingly on the cardinal virtues rather than the Ten Commandments. More use would be made than previously of Old Testament Scripture. Catholic clergy and laity would be permitted and even encouraged to participate in ecumenical services with those of other denominations.

Religious orders were called upon to return to the spirit of the Gospel and to the specific vision of their founder: they would radically change or discard their habits (out went such items as the coif, the guimp, the dimity and the cincture); and they would reassess their roles and functions. The Sisters of Mercy, for example, founded by Catherine McAuley in Dublin to minister to the poor, began to question whether they should be teaching the daughters of the New Zealand middle-class to rise higher on the social and economic ladder. Some decided that they should not be and left their convents — but not their order — to work among the contemporary destitute and disadvantaged. There were also major changes in wider Church organisations: priests' senates; diocesan pastoral councils; a national commission for the laity; a Commission for Peace, Justice and Development to advise bishops on social justice issues; and parish pastoral councils working in partnership with priests to 'share in the priesthood of Christ'.

For bishops, clergy, religious and laity, these changes amounted to a religious revolution: an alteration in the structure and culture of the Church, locally and internationally, on a scale unseen since the Reformation. Some coped better than others. Peter McKeefrey, proclaimed New Zealand's first Cardinal in 1968, uncomfortable in the role of reformer, was succeeded in 1974 as Archbishop of Wellington and Metropolitan by Reginald Delargy. Delargy was made Cardinal in turn in 1976. The role of visionary among the hierarchy passed to Brian Ashby, the energetic and charismatic Bishop of Christchurch, who was to take a lead on social justice issues, particularly those involving Maori–Pakeha relations, overseas aid and sporting contacts with South Africa (which he visited, to see for himself the consequences of Apartheid). The effect of his leadership was visible in 1981, when scarcely a priest in his diocese supported that year's tour by the Springbok rugby team.

Some clergy and religious found the pace of ecclesiastical change too rapid; for others it was too slow. A consequence of both responses was that a proportion of men and women left their posts to work in the secular world (5 percent of clergy in the Auckland Diocese resigned over an eight-year period). Congregations were depleted also by laity who chose to leave the Church on both liberal and conservative grounds; or because they were confused by the onrush of new ideas and the sight of nuns wearing secular dresses with rising hemlines. The broad stream of New Zealand Catholics, however, according to one observer, 'did their best to follow the Church's lead, loyally accepting new ways and trying to get used to them'. Indeed, some saw the decline in religious 'professionals' as an opportunity to assume many religious tasks — in liturgy and education — formerly carried out by religious and priests. The drop in the number of vocations and the movement of many religious out of teaching meant that lay teachers steadily took over the running of Catholic schools, which were then integrated into the State system in the 1970s; in church, lay men and women were authorised to distribute Communion.

Throughout this period Catholicism in New Zealand ceased to be an offspring of the Irish diaspora and became something much more like an indigenous Church. The number of Irish-born clergy and religious fell as they died or retired and were not replaced by their compatriots. Increasing use was made of Maori and New Zealand English in the liturgy. Prayers, hymns, and regalia incorporated New Zealand references and motifs. The number of Maori clergy rose sharply — to nine in the 1990s — and a Maori Catholic bishop, Max Takuira Mariu, was consecrated in 1988 as a consequence of Maori Catholics lobbying the Vatican. In 1986 a reigning Pope, John Paul II, visited New Zealand and was adorned with a Maori feather cloak and pectoral cross of pounamu. By that time, all the Catholic hierarchy were New Zealand-born, and two new dioceses had been created based on Hamilton and Palmerston North.

The post-Vatican II bishops were not the frosty 'Princes of the Church' that some of their predecessors had seemed. John Mackey, John Rodgers, Denis Browne and Pat Dunn in Auckland, Eddie Gaines, Max Mariu and Denis Browne in Hamilton, Peter Cullinane and Owen Dolan in Palmerston North, Cardinal Tom Williams and John Dew in Wellington, John Cunneen in Christchurch, Len Boyle in Dunedin — all were warm, approachable men, respected and liked by their laity and clergy. Priests too found their role altered in the new era: whereas previously that role had been 'private and functionary', exercisers of rubrics who gave instruction to their flock, they were now required to work in partnership with their congregations. It was as if in coming to face their people they had themselves to acquire a personality. Some made the transition with ease and grace, others with difficulty; and a few not at all.

The pace of change, so much more rapid than the peaceful, slow reordering of the Church originally envisaged by the bishops in Council, also brought stress. In some parishes and at least one diocese the balance in the new partnership of priest and congregation, bishop and flock, was not found without disagreement and pain. Women, some of them lay and many of them members of religious orders who had moved from teaching into pastoral and social work, required that their presence and their talents be given more acknowledgement and affirmation than had been the case in the pre-Council Church. The nature of women's ministry within the local Church was debated in the early 1990s through a report of the New Zealand Bishop's Conference entitled 'Made in God's Image'; and that debate at times provoked conflict and grief. The question of the need for clerical celibacy was raised increasingly in public discussion as it was in other parts of the Catholic world; again, the discussion generated a degree of conflict. The New Zealand Church, like the international Church, was having to learn to reconcile honesty, directness and diversity with compassion and respect.

By the 1980s Maori too were asking more questions about their place in the New Zealand Church, and about the extent to which they could retain their values and rituals and still be full members of a worldwide hierarchical institution. The appointment of the Maori Bishop went some way towards reassuring them that the structure and theology of the local Church could embrace tikanga Maori; as did the establishment of Te Runanga o te Hahi Katorika to advise the bishops on Maori spiritual and pastoral matters, and the recognition of diocesan synods that the relationship between Pakeha and Maori was one of partnership, founded in religious principles, social equity and the Treaty of Waitangi. But the location of Max Mariu's bishopric in the diocese of

Hamilton diminished the sense in which he could be regarded as a bishop to and for all Maori, and left some Maori feeling that the New Zealand Church was not yet ready to fully embrace the country's indigenous people.

Another feature of the post-Conciliar Church in New Zealand was an increase in the numbers of Catholics who were neither Irish nor Maori in origin. In Auckland in the 1990s, for example, Mass was celebrated regularly in Chinese, Croatian, Filipino, Indian, Indonesian, Korean, Polish, Spanish, Vietnamese, Tongan, Samoan, and Cook Islands Maori. It was estimated that by the year 2000 these minority groups would make up more than half the Catholic population of the diocese.

As it had done in previous eras, the post-Council Church in New Zealand threw up people whose quest for equity and social justice was driven by their religious principles. Some of these became national figures: poet and social critic James K. Baxter, Maori activists Manuka Henare and Tipene O'Regan, the Consedine brothers Robert and Jim, peace campaigner Moana Cole, and Mercy Sister Pauline O'Regan, who shared her transition from convent community to urban social work in a series of engaging books. Catholics continued their involvement in public life and, in the 1990s, included three political party leaders — Jim Bolger, Jim Anderton and Peter Dunne; and Bolger had been the country's fourth Catholic Prime Minister. Some of the most politically active women — including Ruth Richardson and Lianne Dalziel — also had Catholic backgrounds. In contrast with the sectarian atmosphere that had prevailed seventy years earlier, however, religion had ceased to be a political issue, other than as an aspect of the continuing discussion over levels of State funding of private schools or as an adjunct to the debate on abortion.

A new generation of Catholic writers emerged too in the post-Vatican II years. Some, such as Roderick Finlayson, Amelia Batistich and M. K. Joseph, had begun publishing fiction and poetry in earlier decades. A number of the new writers, Vincent O'Sullivan, Fiona Farrell and Anne Kennedy, wrote about New Zealand society at large, though from viewpoints conditioned by their Catholic upbringing. Others, like the convert Baxter, at times addressed specifically religious and spiritual issues: Sam Hunt, Joy Cowley, Elizabeth Smither, Gregory O'Brien, Andrew Johnston and Chris Orsman. Many also raised insistent voices on moral and political issues, such as involvement in the Vietnam War and sporting contacts with South Africa.

The journalist John Kennedy was a forceful advocate for fundamentalist Catholic viewpoints in his more than two-decade reign as editor of the *Tablet* (which closed in 1996 after a 123-year publishing history; *Zealandia* had predeceased it). Others who had used the Catholic and secular media to promote their own brand of Catholic values and perspectives included Professor J. C. Reid of Auckland University, the morals campaigner Patricia Bartlett, and the Marist apologist Father G. H. Duggan, who became one of the country's most prolific writers of letters to the editor. Conservatives by no means held the floor exclusively, however. Responses to their arguments revealed that New Zealand Catholic opinions on social and political issues were as varied as those in the community at large.

By the 1990s around half a million New Zealanders continued to identify themselves as Catholic. This meant they made up between 14 and 15 percent of the total population (behind Anglicans and Presbyterians) — which was the same proportion and position they had occupied one hundred years earlier. If they were not gaining ground numerically, nor were they losing it, though church attendance was falling in most parts of the country. Those who did attend were more committed to their Church, however, and more involved in parish activities than earlier generations of their co-religionists. And nothing seemed more certain than that New Zealand Catholics would continue to play a significant role in national and community life as Christendom approached its third millennium.

ACKNOWLEDGEMENTS

The circumstances in which this book came to be written did not permit extensive research from primary sources, other than for some aspects of Maori Catholicism. Such research is currently all but impossible given the condition of Catholic diocesan archives (with the exception of those in Auckland). So this book is, in effect, an extended and illustrated essay: one person's overview of the New Zealand Catholic community drawn largely from secondary sources. In the terms of my commission, it is written very much for a general readership, not for a scholarly or academic audience.

I was helped especially by the pioneering work of Father Ernest Simmons, with whom I discussed this book at the outset: in particular by his *A Brief History of the Catholic Church in New Zealand*, his history of the Auckland Diocese and his biography of Bishop Pompallier. I have not footnoted heavily, other than when I am quoting directly. Most of the statistics I cite are from one or other of Simmons's books.

Another history I made much use of is that of the Christchurch Diocese by Father Michael O'Meeghan. In addition, Father O'Meeghan was kind enough to read an early draft of the manuscript of this book and to make many suggestions, some of which saved me from elementary errors. A third and unpublished diocesan history, that of Otago by Basil Howard, I was not given access to, though other scholars have been permitted to read it.

Among other historians whose work I have drawn from extensively are Patrick O'Farrell, Hugh Laracy, Rory Sweetman, John Broadbent, John Dunmore and Jessie Munro. My use of their research is acknowledged in the source notes and bibliography. An important book about Catholicism in New Zealand, Rory Sweetman's account of Bishop James Liston's trial for sedition, was published after this one was written, as was Anna Rogers' *A Lucky Landing, The Story of the Irish in New Zealand.*

My other major debts are to Father James Lyons, formerly of Catholic Communications, and Doug Todd of Tablet Colour Print for originally commissioning the book; Geoff Walker of Penguin New Zealand for assuming final responsibility for its publication; Merle van de Klundert for carrying out most of the archival research and answering dozens of queries; and my wife, Maria Jungowska, for massive logistical support, editing the manuscript, and reminding me that the piety and determination of the Irish has been matched only by that of the Poles.

Father Bruce Bolland of Auckland Catholic Diocesan Archives and Brother Gerard Hogg of the Society of Mary's Archives both gave me fraternal encouragement and assistance well beyond the call of duty.

I thank too the late Dame Whina Cooper for sharing with me her vast knowledge of the history of Maori Catholic experience, particularly in the Hokianga; and Fathers Henare Tate and James Durning, Manuka Henare and Gloria Herbert for advice and information on other aspects of Maori Catholic life.

From an earlier period of my life I acknowledge the impact on my religious upbringing made by my mother, Eleanor Frances King, my grandmother, Eleanor Frances Tierney, and Sisters Isidore McLaughlan, Andrew Lysaght and Domitille Reilly of the Sisters of Saint Joseph of Nazareth. I note here too my gratitude for a long and educative association with the Society of Mary, responsible for early Catholic evangelising in New Zealand. Among my early inspirational teachers were Fathers Bernard Ryan, Noel Delaney, Gerald Arbuckle, Bill O'Fagan and George Head. In my tertiary years I had close associations with Fathers Maurice Mulcahy (who gave me my first job in journalism) and Frank McKay, a long-time mentor and friend. Recently, as noted, I have benefited from sound advice from Father Michael O'Meeghan.

Finally, I thank all those others who contributed photographs, documents or other information to this book: Tim Beaglehole, A. C. Bellamy, Father Frank Bennett, Sister Francesca Bourke, Tom and Trish Brooking, Peg Cadigan, L. M. Campbell, Edith Campion, Father Edmund Campion, Simon Cauchi, Father Kevin Clark, Brother Edward Clisby, Robert Consedine, Nina Cuccurullo, Glenys Dalziel, Frank Della Barca, Sister Colleen Dempsey, Sister M. Duchesne, Tom Duffy, Barbara Duggan, Sister Cathy Egan, Paul Elenio, Susan Ellis, Angela Finnerty, Marie Fleury, Peter Gibbons, Jeanine Graham, M. Grayland, George Griffiths, Kath Haliday, Lisl Heller, Des Hill, Richard Hlavac, Louise Hoobin, Des Hurley, Philip Jane, Geraldine Judkins, June Jungowska, E. C. Keating, Father Donal Kerr, Lewis King, Ken

Larsen, Kim Lasenby, Margaret Lawlor, Father Chris Loughnan, Dennis McEldowney, Jill McGruddy, V. McSweeney, Irene Mackle, Bruce Maguire, Patricia Matheson, Dinah Morrison, Keir Morrison, Iris Murphy, Denis O'Brien, Patricia O'Connor, Patricia O'Leary, Sister Pauline O'Regan, Julie Park, Connie Purdue, Peter Quinn, Sue Reidy, Anne Salmond, Colin Salt, Patricia Saville, Leone Shaw, Father Michael Shirres, David Simmons, Dianne Strevens, Mary Stuart, Jim Swann, Mary Thomas, Bill Ward, Maurice Watson, Sister Elizabeth Ward, Father Dennis Whelan, Sister Bernadette Mary Wrack, Father Nicholas Zeyen and members of the Catholic Women's League.

The drawings on pages 32, 33, 122, 128, 136, 143 and 173 are from Peter Buck's *Coming of the Maori*, Maori Purposes Fund Board/Whitcombe and Tombs, Wellington, 1974.

Special thanks to Miss Julia Moriarty for assistance over a long period with illustrations and aspects of the text.

SOURCE NOTES

PROLOGUE
Being Catholic ~ A Memoir

1. Father Edmund Campion, quoted in *Sydney Morning Herald*, 8/9/94.
2. King 1985, pp.45–6.
3. O'Farrell 1990, pp.83–4; the description is actually about Samuel McCaughey of New South Wales, but it applies as well to William Massey.
4. King 1985, p.25.
5. Chesterton 1927, pp.272–3.
6. *Ibid*, p.105.
7. O'Brien 1968, p.7.
8. O'Farrell 1990, p.290.
9. *Ibid*, pp.290-1.
10. *Ibid*, p.88.
11. Prayer of Saint Francis of Assisi beginning, 'Lord, make me an instrument of Your peace'; quoted from memory.
12. *Saint Andrew Daily Missal*, Abbey of Saint Andrew, Belgium, 1958, p.802.
13. *Ibid*, p.811.

CHAPTER ONE
First Footprints

1. Elenio 1995, p.8; and Professor T. H. Beaglehole, p.c. 11/6/96. I am assuming that the Cork, Italian and Brazilian crew members were at least nominally Catholic. Beaglehole comments soberly that in spite of presumed religious affiliation, 'I suspect they were a pretty Godless lot on the whole.'

2. In the words of one historian, this fact is 'probable, not proven' (Michael O'Meeghan, p.c. 9/8/96). The grounds for the probability are discussed further on in the chapter.
3. Salmond 1991, pp.352 & 353.
4. For discussion of these aspects of Maori and Christian cosmology I am indebted to Dame Whina Cooper, Father Henare Tate and Manuka Henare. The foregoing summary is, of course, what I have made of the discussion.
5. Salmond 1991, p.323.
6. For this information on Surville and biographical material on Father Villefeix I have to thank Professor John Dunmore, who turned over to me a file of data collected by him and Father Godfrey Ainsworth; see Dunmore, p.c. 14/10/93.
7. Salmond 1991, p.321.
8. Dunmore, p.c. 14/10/93.
9. Salmond 1991, pp.340 & 343.
10. See Broadbent 1993, p.19.
11. Campion 1987, p.12.
12. For most of this data on Dillon and Solages I am indebted to Davidson 1975.
13. *Ibid*, pp.237–8.
14. Simmons 1978, p.8.
15. *Ibid*, p.10.
16. Campion 1987, p.4. He is writing here of early Catholicism in Australia; but his comments are equally valid applied to Catholics in New Zealand in the 1820s and 1830s. The point should be made, however, that the post-Famine Irish who found their way to New Zealand in the course of the South Island and Coromandel gold rushes, and as part of the Vogel-inspired immigration schemes, were far better educated in the beliefs and practices of the Catholic Church.
17. See *Zealandia*, 11/1/81; letter to Ernest Simmons from Lois McCarthy (a Poynton descendant), 1/2/81, held by Auckland Diocesan Archives; and Laracy 1995, p.3.
18. Copy of undated letter from Thomas Poynton to Cardinal Moran held by Wellington Diocesan Archives.
19. *Marist Messenger*, 1/3/38, p.66; Father Henare Tate and Manuka Henare both made the point to me in personal communications that this practice of public recitation of the rosary established by the Poyntons remained strong among Hokianga Maori long after the Poyntons had left the district.
20. Simmons 1984, p.16
21. *Ibid*, p.16.
22. See Larkin 1995.

23. It was Whina Cooper who quoted this proverb to me in association with the arrival of the schooner *Raiatea*, interview Panguru, 11/11/82.
24. Again, the source is Whina Cooper.
25. Simmons 1978, p.11.
26. Nathaniel Turner, quoted in Davidson/Lineham 1987, p.49.
27. Broadbent 1993, p.20.
28. Simmons 1984, p.36.
29. *Ibid*, pp.35–6.
30. W. Williams to E. G. Marsh, 8/3/39; quoted in Simmons 1984, p.41.
31. Poynton Ms p.8; and Simmons 1978, p.12.
32. Moran 1897, pp.898 & 899.
33. Servant, C., *Customs and Habits of the New Zealanders 1838–42*, Wellington 1973.
34. Garin to Meximieux, 12/6/41; quoted in Simmons 1984, p.58.
35. Simmons 1978, p.18.
36. Moran 1897, p.904.
37. Chouvet 1985, pp.70–1.
38. This story is an established part of Catholic Maori oral tradition. It was recounted to me over the years by Father G. Arbuckle, David Simmons and Manuka Henare. Written versions of it can be found in Arbuckle 1976 and Manuka Henare, *Tablet*, 18/12/85, p.6. Some of its details — who the priest was and precisely which chapel was involved — have not been verified.
39. See for example Michael O'Meeghan in 'Connexions' programme on Bishop Pompallier, Radio New Zealand, 5/12/93; and see Pompallier's 'instructions to his assistants' in Davidson/Lineham 1987, pp.50–1.
40. Simmons 1984, p.60.
41. The traveller is Ensign Best; see Simmons 1978, p.23.
42. Davidson/Lineham 1987, p.51.

CHAPTER TWO
A French Church?

1. For information on the Akaroa colony and the fate of its priests I am indebted to Tremewan 1990, especially pp.250–4; and O'Meeghan 1988.
2. Most sources give the name of the vessel from which Father Borjon and Brother Déodat drowned as the *Eleanor*; but this is a result of a mistake made by Pompallier. The vessel concerned was the *Speculator* (Michael O'Meeghan, p.c., 9/8/96).

3. O'Sullivan 1977, p.11 (although Burns 1989 says that the first wearing of Father O'Reily's wig occurred the day the *Thomas Sparkes* arrived in Wellington, 31/1/43 p.196).
4. O'Sullivan 1977, p.18; I have drawn all my information on Father O'Reily from O'Sullivan's small biography of the Irish priest.
5. *Ibid*, p.38.
6. *Ibid*, p.47.
7. Ewart 1989, p.12.
8. This incident was much discussed among Tainui tribes in the latter part of the nineteenth and early twentieth centuries. See King 1977, especially Chapter 10.
9. Manuka Henare, p.c., 6/9/96.
10. Simmons 1978, p.40.
11. Simmons 1990, p.350.
12. Simmons 1984, pp.156–7.
13. This is Simmons's judgment and, while some have disputed it (for example Michael O'Meeghan, p.c., 9/8/96), it is the only conclusion one can draw from the movement of personnel at the relevant times.
14. King 1977, p.174.
15. Munro 1996, p.101.
16. Simmons 1978, p.49.
17. This story is still told among Catholic Maori of the Whanganui. See also Munro 1996, p.149.
18. Harris 1994, p.41.
19. Father Chataigner to his brother, 19/11/60, Marist Archives.
20. Simmons 1978, p.58.
21. See Condon 1986, p.318; and Simmons 1978, p.56.
22. Munro 1996, p.108.
23. Clisby 1993, pp.17–18.

CHAPTER THREE
An Irish Church

1. Simmons 1982, p.119.
2. Broadbent 1990, p.26.
3. *Ibid*, p.26; and Laracy 1993, p.334.
4. Simmons 1981, p.154.
5. Simmons 1978, p.67.
6. *Ibid*, pp.78–9.
7. Redwood 1922 (part 2), pp.23–4.
8. King 1985, p.57.
9. See Bruce Ansley's article 'In the Brothers' keeping', *Listener*, 4/12/93, pp.24–6; letter from David Ross of

Catholic Communications, *Listener*, 15/1/94; and Michael O'Meeghan, p.c., 16/8/96.
10. Simmons 1978, pp.82–3.
11. Simmons 1981, p.29.
12. *Ibid*, p.29.
13. Laracy 1996, p.259
14. *Ibid*, p.259.
15. O'Farrell 1990, p.87.
16. Simmons 1978, p.87.
17. Simmons, unpublished biographical card index, Auckland Catholic Archives.
18. N. A. Simmons 1981, pp.179–80.
19. *Ibid*, p.151.
20. Oddly, Munro 1996 does not deal with this consequence of Suzanne Aubert's career. But anybody brought up Catholic in New Zealand in the 1940s and 1950s heard whispers — from priests and nuns — of the likelihood of Mother Aubert's canonisation.
21. See O'Meeghan 1988, Chapter 11.
22. *Ibid*, pp.343–4; the address written for Fr Foley on his departure is held in St Theresa's presbytery, Waitangi, Chatham Island.
23. Ewart 1989, p.39.
24. Simmons 1978, p.77.
25. *Ibid*, p.90.
26. *Ibid*, p.94.
27. Simmons 1982, p.218.
28. Simmons 1978, p.98.
29. Sweetman July 1993 ('Bishop in the dock'), p.220.
30. *Ibid*, p.221.
31. Felix Kane, Supreme Knight, p.c. 25/11/93 & 4/2/94.
32. Bishop Matthew Brodie's investigation of the Cleary–Liston dispute, Christchurch Catholic Archives, pp.1 & 3.
33. Simmons 1978, p.97.
34. *Ibid*, pp.100–101.
35. McKay 1977, p.21.
36. *Ibid*, p.31.
37. Ovenden 1996, p.5.
38. Dan Davin, *Selected Stories*, Wellington, 1981, p.22.
39. *Ibid*, p.23.
40. Michael King, *Frank Sargeson, A Life*, Auckland, 1995, p.247, and Maurice Duggan, *Collected Stories*, Auckland, 1981, p.29.
41. Park 1992, p.25.
42. O'Meeghan 1988, pp.260–61.
43. See Munro 1996.

44. For information on Francis Vernon Douglas I am indebted to a variety of personal communications from Patricia Brooks; and to several articles by her, including *Tablet* 7/2/96, p.13.
45. Edith Campion in *The Book of New Zealand Women*, Wellington, 1991, p.195.
46. Interview with Fr Frank Bennett, Tairua, 11/8/95.
47. Simmons 1978, p.104.
48. Information on CYM in addition to that from Bennett and Simmons comes from Desmond Hurley, p.c., 23/3/96.
49. Simmons 1978, p.105; and O'Meeghan 1988, p.265 (although O'Meeghan rates Lyons rather better than Simmons on the bishop's relations with laity).
50. I was living in the Auckland Diocese in the 1960s and early 1970s and saw first hand the effects of Archbishop Liston's conservatism. The phrase 'creeping infallibility' is that of a priest, whose anonymity I have agreed to protect.
51. See King 1983.

❖

SELECT BIBLIOGRAPHY

Akenson, Donald Harmon, *Half the World From Home, Perspectives on the Irish in New Zealand 1860–1850*, Wellington, 1990

Arbuckle, Gerald, *The Church in a Multi-Cultural Society*, Wellington, 1976

Audacity of Faith, Sisters of Compassion Centennial 1892–1992, Wellington, 1992

Barber, Laurie, 'John Patrick Fitzgerald, doctor, community leader, hospital superintendent' in *Dictionary of New Zealand Biography, vol.1, 1769–1869*, Wellington, 1990, pp.128–9

Broadbent, John, 'Antoine Marie Garin, priest, missionary, educationalist' in *Dictionary of New Zealand Biography, vol.1, 1769–1869*, Wellington, 1990, pp.144–5

Broadbent, John, 'Francis William Redwood, Catholic archbishop' in *Dictionary of New Zealand Biography, vol.2, 1870–1900*, Wellington, 1993, pp.406–8

Broadbent, John, 'Philippe Joseph Viard, priest, missionary, bishop' in *Dictionary of New Zealand Biography, vol.1, 1769–1869*, Wellington, 1990, pp.560–1

Broadbent, John, 'Catholicism' in *The Farthest Jerusalem, Four Lectures on the Origins of Christianity in Otago*, Dunedin, 1993, pp.19–29

Burns, Patricia, *Fatal Success, A History of the New Zealand Company*, Auckland, 1989

Campion, Edmund, *Australian Catholics*, Melbourne, 1987

Campion, Edmund, *A Place in the City*, Melbourne, 1994

Chesterton, G. K., *The Collected Poems of G. K. Chesterton*, London, 1927

Chouvet, J. A. M., *A Marist Missionary in New Zealand 1843–1846*, Whakatane, 1985

Church, Ian, 'Jean Lampila, missionary' in *Dictionary of New Zealand Biography, vol.1, 1769–1869*, Wellington, 1990, p.235

Clisby, Edward, 'Our martyrs, Brother Euloge' in *Marist News*, November 1993, pp.17–18

Condon, Kevin, *The Missionary College of All Hallows 1842–1891*, Dublin, 1986

Davidson, Allan K. & Lineham, Peter J., *Transplanted Christianity, Documents Illustrating Aspects of New Zealand Church History*, Palmerston North, 1987

Davidson, J. W., *Peter Dillon of Vanikoro, Chevalier of the South Seas*, Melbourne, 1975

Davis, Richard P., *Irish Issues in New Zealand Politics 1868–1922*, Dunedin, 1974

De Courcy, Noeline, *Catholic Women's League of New Zealand, National History 1931–1990*, Dunedin, 1990

Delany, Veronica, 'Mary Cecilia Maher, nun, teacher, social worker' in *Dictionary of New Zealand Biography, vol.1, 1769–1869*, Wellington, 1990, pp.259–60

Donovan, Peter (ed.), *Religions of New Zealanders*, Palmerston North, 1990

Dunmore, John (ed.), *New Zealand and the French, Two Centuries of Contact*, Waikanae, 1990

Dunmore, John (ed.), *The French and the Maori*, Waikanae, 1992

Elenio, Paul, *Alla Fine Del Mondo, To the Ends of the Earth, A History of Italian Immigration to the Wellington Region*, Wellington, 1995

Ewart, Peter, *Aspects of the Apostolates of the Society of Mary in New Zealand*, Wellington, 1989

Gallagher, Pat, *The Marist Brothers in New Zealand, Fiji and Samoa 1876–1976*, Auckland, 1976

Gardiner, Paul, *Mary MacKillop, An Extraordinary Australian*, Alexandria, 1994

Goulter, Mary C., *Sons of France: A Forgotten Influence on New Zealand History*, Wellington, 1958

Gracious is the Time, Centenary of Sisters of Mercy, Auckland New Zealand, 1850–1950, Auckland, 1952

Graham, Jeanine, *Frederick Weld*, Auckland, 1983

Graham, Judith, *Breaking the Habit: Life in a New Zealand Dominican Convent, 1955–1967*, Dunedin, 1992

Harris, Anthony, *The Beauty of Your House, The Nelson Catholic Parish*, Nelson, 1994

Jackson, H. R., *Churches and People in Australia and New Zealand 1860–1930*, Wellington, 1987

Keyes, L. G., *The Life and Times of Bishop Pompallier*, Christchurch, 1957

Keyes, L. G., *Philippe Viard, Bishop of Wellington*, Christchurch, 1968

King, Michael, *Te Puea*, Auckland, 1977

King, Michael, *Whina, A Biography of Whina Cooper*, Auckland, 1983

King, Michael, *Being Pakeha, An Encounter with New Zealand and*

the Maori Renaissance, Auckland, 1985
Kinsella, Paddy, Mackle, Irene, & Molloy, Brendan, *Pukekaraka*, Levin, 1994
Laracy, Hugh M., 'Bishop Moran, Irish politics and Catholicism in New Zealand' in *Journal of Religious History* 6, no.1 (1970), pp.62–76
Laracy, Hugh M., 'From Maori Mission to Settler Church, New Zealand Catholicism in the mid-nineteenth century' in *New Hope for Our Society*, 1985
Laracy, Hugh M., 'Patrick Moran, Catholic Bishop' in *Dictionary of New Zealand Biography, vol.2, 1870–1900*, Wellington, 1993, pp.333–5
Laracy, Hugh M., 'Les Pères Mariste and New Zealand: the Irish connection' in R. P. Davies (ed.), *Irish Australian Studies, Papers delivered at the Eight Irish–Australian Conference*, July 1995
Laracy, Hugh M., 'Martin Kennedy, merchant, mine owner, businessman, Catholic layman' in *Dictionary of New Zealand Biography, vol.3, 1901–1920*, Wellington, 1996, p.259
Larkin, Craig, *A Certain Way, An Exploration of Marist Spirituality*, Rome, 1995
McCarthy, Mary Augustine, *Star in the South, The Centennial History of New Zealand Dominican Sisters*, Dunedin, 1970
McConnell, Robin, *Taua of Kareponia, Leader from the North*, Hamilton, 1993
McGill, David, *The Lion and the Wolfhound, The Irish Rebellion on the New Zealand Goldfields*, Wellington, 1990
McHardy, Emmet, *Blazing the Trail*, Sydney, 1935
McKay, Frank, *Eileen Duggan*, Wellington, 1977
McKay, Frank, *The Life of James K. Baxter*, Auckland, 1990
McKeefrey, Peter, *Fishers of Men*, Auckland, 1938
Maguire, Bruce, *Catholic Education in Gisborne 1894–1994*, Gisborne, 1994
Mill Hill Fathers, *Our Maori Mission*, Auckland, 1933
Moran, Patrick Francis, *History of the Catholic Church in Australasia*, Sydney, 1897
Munro, Jessie, *The Story of Suzanne Aubert*, Auckland, 1996
O'Brien, John, *Around the Boree Log and other verses*, Sydney, 1968
O'Farrell, Patrick, *Vanished Kingdoms, Irish in Australia and New Zealand*, Sydney, 1990
O'Farrell, Patrick, *Through Irish Eyes, Australian and New Zealand Images of the Irish 1788–1948*, Richmond, 1994
Oliver, Steven, 'Heremia Te Wake, Te Rarawa leader, farmer, assessor, catechist' in *Dictionary of New Zealand Biography, vol.2, 1870–1900*, Wellington, 1993, p.528

O'Meeghan, Michael, *Held Firm by Faith, A History of the Catholic Diocese of Christchurch 1840–1987*, Christchurch, 1988

O'Meeghan, Michael, 'Catholic beginnings in New Zealand, an overview' in *Christian Brethren Research Fellowship Journal* 121, 1990, pp.29–34

O'Meeghan, Michael, 'John Joseph Grimes, Catholic bishop' in *Dictionary of New Zealand Biography, vol.2, 1870–1900*, Wellington, 1993, pp.179–80

O'Regan, Pauline, *A Changing Order*, Wellington, 1987

O'Regan, Pauline, *Aunts and Windmills, Stories from My Past*, Wellington, 1991

O'Regan, Pauline, *There is Hope for a Tree*, Wellington, 1995

O'Sullivan, Owen, *Apostle in Aotearoa, A Biography of Father Jeremiah Joseph Purcell O'Reily, OFM Cap. Wellington's First Catholic Pastor*, Auckland, 1977

Ovenden, Keith, *A Fighting Withdrawal, The Life of Dan Davin, Writer, Soldier, Publisher*, Oxford, 1996

Park, Ruth, *A Fence Around the Cuckoo*, Melbourne, 1992

Pobog-Jaworowski, J. W., *History of the Polish Settlers in New Zealand 1776–1987*, Warsaw, 1990

Power, Anne Marie, *Sisters of St Joseph of the Sacred Heart, New Zealand Story 1883–1983*, Auckland, 1983

Rafter, Pat, *Never Let Go! The Remarkable Story of Mother Aubert*, Wellington, 1972

Redwood, Francis, *Reminiscences of Early Days in New Zealand* (parts one & two), Wellington, 1922

Riseborough, Hazel, 'Ottavio Barsanti, missionary, priest, writer' in *Dictionary of New Zealand Biography, vol.1, 1769–1869*, Wellington, 1990, pp.21–2

Roach, Kevin, 'The Growth of Roman Catholicism in New Zealand' in *Religion in New Zealand*, Wellington, 1990, pp.111–36

Ross, Ruth, 'The Maori Church in Northland' in *Historic Buildings of New Zealand, North Island*, Auckland, 1979

Salmond, Anne, *Two Worlds, First Meetings Between Maori and Europeans 1642–1772*, Auckland, 1991

Servant, C., *Customs and Habits of the New Zealanders 1838–42*, Wellington, 1973

Simmons, E. R., *A Brief History of the Catholic Church in New Zealand*, Auckland, 1978

Simmons, E. R., *In Cruce Salus, A History of the Diocese of Auckland 1848–1980*, Auckland, 1982

Simmons, E. R., *Pompallier, Prince of Bishops*, Auckland, 1984

Simmons, E. R., 'Jean-Baptiste François Pompallier, bishop, missionary' in *Dictionary of New Zealand Biography, vol.1, 1769–1869*, Wellington, 1990, pp.349–50

Simmons, Nicholas Anthony, 'Archbishop Francis Redwood, his

contribution to Catholicism in New Zealand', unpublished MA thesis, Massey University, 1981

Smithies, Ruth, *Ten Steps Towards Bicultural Action, A Handbook on Partnership in Aotearoa–New Zealand*, Wellington 1990

The Story of Mill Hill in New Zealand, Putaruru, 1966

Strevens, Dianne M., 'The Sisters of St Joseph of Nazareth, New Zealand, 1880–1965', unpublished Master of Theology thesis, Melbourne College of Divinity, 1995

Sweetman, Rory, 'Research on New Zealand Catholicism, What? Where? Who? Why?' in *Archifacts*, October 1990, pp.28–32

Sweetman, Rory, 'Bishop in the dock, the sedition trial of James Liston' in *Irish–Australian Studies*, July 1993, pp.218–27

Sweetman, Rory, 'Thomas William Croke, Catholic bishop' in *Dictionary of New Zealand Biography, vol.2, 1870–1900*, Wellington, 1993, pp.104–5

Sweetman, Rory, 'Henry William Cleary, Catholic bishop, editor, army chaplain' in *Dictionary of New Zealand Biography, vol.3, 1901–1920*, Wellington, 1996, pp.101–3

Sweetman, Rory, 'James Joseph Kelly, Catholic priest, editor' in *Dictionary of New Zealand Biography, vol.3, 1901–1920*, Wellington, 1996, pp.256–7

Tennant, M. A., 'Mary Joseph Aubert, Catholic nun, nurse, herbalist, teacher, social worker, writer' in *Dictionary of New Zealand Biography, vol.2, 1870–1900*, Wellington, 1993, pp.16–19

Tremewan, Peter, *French Akaroa, An Attempt to Colonise Southern New Zealand*, Christchurch, 1990

Turner, Philip, 'Louis Catherin Servant, priest, missionary' in *Dictionary of New Zealand Biography, vol.1, 1769–1869*, Wellington, 1990, pp.389–90.

Van der Krogt, Christopher, 'Thomas O'Shea, Catholic archbishop' in *Dictionary of New Zealand Biography, vol.3, 1901–1920*, Wellington, 1996, pp.374–5

Vaney, Neil, 'William John Larkin' in *Dictionary of New Zealand Biography, vol.1, 1769–1869*, Wellington, 1990, pp.236–7

Whiteford, Peter (ed.), *Eileen Duggan, Selected Poems*, Wellington, 1994

Williams, Mark (ed.), *The Source of the Song, New Zealand Writers on Catholicism*, Wellington, 1995

INDEX